RELIGIONS OF THE
HELLENISTIC-ROMAN AGE

Religions of the Hellenistic-Roman Age

ANTONÍA TRIPOLITIS

WILLIAM B. EERDMANS PUBLISHING COMPANY
GRAND RAPIDS, MICHIGAN / CAMBRIDGE, U.K.

Wm. B. Eerdmans Publishing Co.
255 Jefferson Ave. S.E., Grand Rapids, Michigan 49503 /
P.O. Box 163, Cambridge CB3 9PU U.K.

Printed in the United States of America

06 05 04 03 02   7 6 5 4 3 2 1

Library of Congress Cataloging-in-Publication Data

Tripolitis, Antonía, 1934-
Religions of the Hellenistic-Roman age / Antonía Tripolitis.
p.   cm.
Includes bibliographical references.
ISBN 0-8028-4913-X (pbk.: alk. paper)
1. Greece — Religon. 2. Rome — Religion.   I. Title.

BT722.T75   2002
200'.938 — dc21

2001040380

www.eerdmans.com

CONTENTS

I. THE HELLENISTIC-ROMAN WORLD   9

A brief historical survey of the development of the Hellenistic-Roman
Age: Alexander's cosmopolitan vision, how it altered the cultural and
sociopolitical systems of the time, and society's religious response to
the changes brought about by Alexander's universalism. The chapter
includes a discussion of the principal mystery cults — Demeter, Dionysus, Isis, Cybele (Magna Mater) — and religious philosophies —
Stoicism, Epicureanism, and Middle Platonism — that developed or
were revitalized during this time.

II. MITHRAISM   47

A study of the cult of Mithras, its origins in Vedic, India, its mystery rites, and its migration throughout the Mediterranean world. Emphasis will be on the social and psychological factors that caused it to develop into a full-fledged, popular religion, and the reasons for its subsequent decline and disappearance.

III. HELLENISTIC JUDAISM   61

The chapter will begin with a historical overview of the Jewish Diaspora from the Babylonian Exile (587 B.C.E.) to the Roman conquest (63 B.C.E.–135 C.E.). It will concentrate on the Hellenization of Diaspora Judaism that began in 333 B.C.E., its cultural and social factors, and the development of Hellenistic Jewish literature, theology, and philosophy; the importance and development of the Hellenistic Jewish synagogue, its art and liturgy, and its influence on Christian church structure and liturgy. Special attention will be given to Philo Judaeus (ca. 30 B.C.E.–45 C.E.), the most outstanding representative of Hellenistic Judaism, his thought, works, and influence on the development of Christian doctrine.

CONTENTS

IV. CHRISTIANITY   91

An examination of the cultural and social milieu in which Christianity emerged, developed, and spread; the pagan opposition to the spread of Christianity and its criticism of the Christian beliefs; the dialogue that ensued between the two groups for three centuries; and the influence of this dialogue on Christianity's evolution as an organization with its own philosophy and tradition. The chapter concludes with a discussion of the social and psychological reasons for Christianity's success.

V. GNOSTICISM   119

An explanation of the term *gnosis* and its usage during the period under discussion; an examination of the social and political factors for Gnosticism's origin and development, its psychological appeal during the first three centuries C.E., and the reasons for its disappearance at the end of the 3rd century. The chapter will investigate the main tenets basic to all gnostic groups, and will discuss the principal Christian (Basilidean, Marcion and Valentinian) and non-Christian (Hermetic gnostic) thought systems.

VI. SUMMARY   143

ABBREVIATIONS

AGJU	*Arbeiten zur Geschichte des antiken Judentums und des Urchristentums*
ANRW	*Aufstieg und Niedergang der römischen Welt*
CRINT	Compendia rerum iudaicarum ad Novum Testamentum
EPRO	Études préliminaires aux religions orientales dans l'empire romain
GRBS	*Greek, Roman, and Byzantine Studies*
HTR	*Harvard Theological Review*
JMS	*Journal of Mithraic Studies*
JRS	*Journal of Roman Studies*
NHL	James M. Robinson, *The Nag Hammadi Library*
OTL	Old Testament Library
SBLDS	Society of Biblical Literature Dissertation Series
SBT	Studies in Biblical Theology
SJLA	Studies in Judaism in Late Antiquity
VC	*Vigiliae christianae*

Ancient Writings

Apuleius *Metam.*	*Metamorphoses*
Cicero *Leg.*	*De legibus*
Clement *Paed.*	*Paedagogus (Tutor)*
Strom.	*Stromata (Miscellanies)*

Corp. herm.	*Corpus hermeticum (Hermetica)*
Euripides *Bacch.*	*Bacchae*
Eusebius *Hist. eccl.*	*Historia ecclesiastica (Ecclesiastical History)*
Herodotus *Hist.*	*Histories*
Hippolytus *Haer.*	*Refutatio omnium haeresium*
Irenaeus *Haer.*	*Adversus haereses*
Justin *1, 2 Apol.*	*Apologia i, ii*
Dial.	*Dialogus cum Tryphone (Dialogue with Trypho)*
Origen *Cels.*	*Contra Celsum*
Comm. Jo.	*Commentarii in evangelium Joannis*
Enarrat. Job	*Enarrationes in Job*
Hom. Num	*Homiliae in Numeros*
Princ.	*De principiis*
Philo *Abr.*	*De Abrahamo*
Cher.	*De cherubim*
Conf.	*De confusione linguarum*
Det.	*Quod deterius potiori insidari soleat*
Ebr.	*De ebrietate*
Flacc.	*In Flaccum*
Fug.	*De fuga et inventione*
Gig.	*De gigantibus*
Her.	*Quis rerum divinarum heres sit*
Leg.	*Legum allegoriae*
Legat.	*Legatio ad Gaium*
Migr.	*De migratione Abrahami*
Mos.	*De vita Mosis*
Opif.	*De opificio mundi*
Plant.	*De plantatione*
Post.	*De posteritate Caini*
Praem.	*De praemiis et poenis*
QE	*Quaestiones et solutiones in Exodum*
QG	*Quaestiones et solutiones in Genesin*
Sacr.	*De sacrificiis Abelis et Caini*
Somn.	*De somniis*
Spec.	*De specialibus legibus*
Virt.	*De virtutibus*
Pindar *Pyth.*	*Pythian Odes*
Tertullian *Marc.*	*Adversus Marcionem (Against Marcion)*

INTRODUCTION

In 331 B.C.E., Alexander of Macedon conquered the Persian Darius III at Gaugamela and proceeded to become master of the far-flung Persian Empire. By the time of his death in 323, Alexander had left an empire stretching from the Aegean eastward to the Indus River in India and from the northern shores of the Black Sea south to Nubia and the Sahara in northern Africa.

Alexander's thirst for territory was not motivated solely by a desire for military power. He also had a goal of establishing an *oikoumene*, a common world, a close-knit, self-contained entity united by the Greek language and culture, but shaped and adapted to a new environment. His empire irreversibly altered the socio-political world of the Mediterranean and Near East. It brought together Greek and oriental, East and West into a culturally unified empire. Provincialism gave way to universalism and collectivism to individualism. The most diverse populations of the Mediterranean and Near Eastern world embraced this new culture. Even the Jewish people, who had always resisted external influences, were not immune from Hellenization, as the new culture came to be called.

The term "Hellenistic" is generally used to refer to the period of history from 331 B.C.E. when Alexander of Macedon defeated the Persian Darius up to Octavius's defeat of Antony and Cleopatra at Actium in 31 B.C.E. Although politically the Hellenistic world came to an end in 31-30 B.C.E., the Hellenistic age continued to flourish under Roman political domination to the extent that it has often been said that "captive Greece captivated her conqueror." Influences of Hellenistic culture are evident up to the Renaissance period. In the study of Hellenistic religions, however, the period ends in the 4th century C.E. with the emergence of the Christian state. In this study, the term "Hellenistic" is used to designate the period from 331 B.C.E., the inauguration of Alexander's empire, to 31 B.C.E., Octavius's victory at Actium; "Hellenistic-Roman" designates period from 30 B.C.E. to the 4th century C.E. and the emergence of the Christian world.

The Hellenistic-Roman age was an era of insecurity and anxiety. The shift from nationalism to cosmopolitanism, from the secure isolated city-state to the *oikoumene,* gave people a greater sense of individualism, but at the same time provided many with a feeling of alienation and insecurity. As people became more mobile and individualistic, old traditions and values were steadily being uprooted, static class structures began to disappear, past certitudes were questioned, and the future became uncertain. By the 2nd century of the present era, the Hellenistic-Roman world had witnessed a succession of barbarian invasions, bloody civil wars, various recurring plagues, famines, and economic crises. Moreover, confidence in the traditional cults and their gods that served as the basis of the political, social, and intellectual life was waning. The general populace no longer placed its hope or faith on the ancient gods, whom they believed could not alleviate their daily encounters with the vicissitudes of Hellenistic life. Although ruler cults were established to replace the traditional city-gods, they were primarily a political phenomenon and did not fulfill the needs of the individual. This was a period of general material and moral insecurity. The unsettling conditions of the time led people to long and search for *soteria,* salvation, a release from the burdens of finitude, the misery and failure of human life. People everywhere were keenly awake to every new message of hope and eagerly prospecting for a personal savior, someone who would bring salvation, i.e., deliverance or protection from the vicissitudes of this life and the perils of the afterlife. This they found in the mystery cults that had penetrated the Greek world.

Although at first they were festivals and celebrations of the seasons, during the Hellenistic-Roman period the mystery cults became a solution to the spiritual needs of the people. With their purification rites, their enthusiasm and ecstasy, and their promising rewards of immortality through deification, the cults satisfied an inner longing for individual salvation, revelation, and redemption, or inner illumination. To the degree that they satisfied the needs of the time, they developed and spread throughout the empire. Some took on a new form as they adapted to the Hellenistic environment. Of the vast number of cults that existed at that time, the more important and popular included the Demeter cult closely associated with the Eleusinian mysteries, the cults of Dionysus, Isis, and Cybele or Magna Mater. The most important of all the cults was that of the oriental sun-deity Mithras. It originated in Vedic, India, migrated to Persia by way of Babylon, and then westward through the Hellenized East, and finally across the length and breadth of the Hellenistic-Roman world. On its westward journey, it incorporated many of the features of the cultures in which it found itself. By the 2nd century C.E., the cult of Mithras had developed into an important Hellenistic mystery religion and, at the beginning of the 4th century, Mithras became the official god of the Roman state. As a religion, Mithraism flourished during the 3rd and 4th centuries. Much of its success was due to its popularity among the Roman soldiers who helped to spread it throughout the empire.

Philosophy was also attempting to meet the needs of the age. Three schools of thought dominated the period, Stoicism, Epicureanism, and a revived Platonism known as Middle Platonism. Stoicism and Epicureanism were new, and they emerged to meet the needs of the time. Revived Platonism re-emerged as a religious philosophy concerned more with the questions and problems of everyday life than with the skeptical theory of knowledge that preoccupied it formerly. These philosophies offered to the educated minority what the mystery cults supplied to the average individual. Their emphasis was on the idea of a single divine First Principle and on the practical and ethical concerns of life, rather than the cosmological and metaphysical speculations of the Classical age. They devoted themselves to the "care of souls," to training individuals how to cope with and to survive in a hostile world.

During this time, Judaism, and in particular the Judaism of the Diaspora, evolved from a state religion to one of the most powerful and widespread of the Hellenistic religions, and from a religion of the book, i.e., the Pentateuch, to a theoretical and philosophical interpretation of its laws and customs. This development is reflected in the Jewish Hellenistic apocalyptic and Wisdom Literature and in the writings of the philosopher Philo, the principal representative of Jewish Hellenistic thought and culture. Philo Judaeus (ca. 20 B.C.E.–50 C.E.) was a thoroughly Hellenized citizen of Alexandria, Egypt, the intellectual and cultural center of the empire and a leader of the large Jewish community of that city. This community was the most important of the Diaspora Jews, one of the first to become Hellenized in both language and culture, and the first to communicate the

3

Jewish faith to the Hellenistic world. In the 3rd century B.C.E., the Alexandrian Jewish community was responsible for the Septuagint, the translation of the Hebrew Scriptures into Greek. The Septuagint became the main factor in the process of the Hellenization of Judaism, and with the spread of Christianity among the Gentiles, beginning in the 1st century C.E., it became an important medium through which the Jewish religious experience was transmitted to the Hellenistic-Roman world. From the 2nd century B.C.E. onwards, the Alexandrian Jews were the link between the Hellenistic-Jewish culture and the Hellenized world, especially through the work of Philo, a correlation of biblical revelation and Greek philosophy. This he accomplished by employing the method of allegorical interpretation. By interpreting the Scriptures allegorically, Philo was able to find in them the contemporary Greek philosophical views that could serve his purpose, to reconcile Hebrew theology with Greek philosophy, while preserving intact the observance of the Old Testament law. His fundamental objective, similar to that of other Jewish Hellenistic writers, was to justify to the Greek-speaking world the claim that Judaism as a philosophy and way of life was older and truer than anything the Greeks were able to offer. Philo's terminology and his use of the allegorical method to interpret Scripture had an enormous influence on the development of early Christian theology.

The Hellenistic-Roman age also witnessed the formation of two major new schools of thought, Christianity and Gnosticism. Christianity was the last major religious movement to develop during the Hellenistic-Roman period. It began as a subgroup within Palestinian Judaism founded by a handful of Jesus' followers who had witnessed his resurrection. They interpreted this event as a sign that Jesus was truly the long sought for Messiah, the expected deliverer or liberator. Christianity was introduced into the Gentile Hellenistic world by the Greek-speaking, missionary-minded Hellenistic Jews who learned of Christianity on their pilgrimages to the temple in Jerusalem during the great religious feasts, especially Passover. Initially Christianity was a movement of the disinherited, the poor, and the uneducated. By the mid-2nd century C.E., it began to recruit members from the intellectual and upper class. In particular, Christianity appealed to the serious students of philosophy who had become disillusioned with the various philosophical schools whose debates led to endless questions but no possible answers. These individuals found in Christianity a genuinely philosophical way of life expressed in simple and direct terms. This is

clearly evident in the works of the early Christian intellectuals who wrote
during the second half of the 2nd century, in the works of Justin Martyr
(ca. 155-160), Tatian (ca. 160-180), and Athenagoras (176-180).

As Christianity continued to gain advocates from all walks of life, its
critics also increased. These included both the Roman authorities and the
pagan intellectuals that it wanted to attract. The Christians' refusal to give
proper homage to the pagan divinities that were considered the emissaries
and helpers of God in ruling the world, and their refusal to bear arms or
participate in civic life, was viewed as revolutionary or seditious. It was
threatening the cohesion and stability of society and the protection of the
empire. Moreover, Christianity was not considered legitimate. It lacked an
established tradition and was completely untenable as a logical process.
Christian beliefs were based on myth. Their teachings were never critically
examined but accepted blindly on faith and not on reason. Christianity
was irrational and had undemonstrated laws. To the educated pagan of the
time, any thought that could not produce reasonable proof of its view
could not produce pious individuals, i.e., moral and ethical individuals
obedient to the state. In defense of Christianity's ideas against its critics,
the Christian intellectuals of the late 2nd century attempted to do for
Christianity what Philo had done earlier for Judaism, to establish it as a
philosophical school. They believed that only by interpreting Christianity
philosophically would it be able to gain acceptance in the Hellenistic-Roman world and to remain faithful to its tradition. Christianity's acceptance
was not readily achieved. Its critics continued to be many and strong, and
this produced a long and vigorous debate between paganism and Christianity. Although the pagan polemics were forceful, Christianity profited
from them. The dialogue between paganism and Christianity introduced a
dialectical element into Christian thinking that helped the Christians to
understand the tradition that they were defending, to systematize their
fundamental beliefs, and to formulate a distinctive Christian teaching. By
the end of the 2nd–early 3rd century, Christianity had firmly established
itself as a recognized religion throughout the empire.

Gnosticism was not a uniform religion. The term is used to refer to a
wide variety of religious views and movements that were influential during the first several centuries C.E., and particularly during the 2nd and 3rd
centuries when the various gnostic teachers dominated Christian intellectual life, each one promulgating his individual views. Gnosticism is a product of Hellenistic syncretism. It is an eclectic fusion of philosophical spec-

5

ulation, astrology, mythology, as well as Egyptian, Persian, Jewish Hellenistic, and Christian ideas. Like many of the other religious ideas of the time, it arose in response to humanity's feelings of insecurity and alienation, which were prevalent at the time. Gnosticism took many forms, ranging from extreme speculations to the crudest fantasies. Through the many varieties of gnostic expression, however, there existed certain common concepts, principal of which was the idea from which the movement received its name, that of *gnosis*, a Greek term meaning knowledge, to which the Gnostics gave a unique meaning. For them, *gnosis* was a special revealed knowledge or revelation that comes from a divine savior who is often understood as Christ. This knowledge, acquired by sudden illumination, enabled the Gnostics to understand the ways of God, the universe and themselves. It was through this special *gnosis*, not through faith, that an individual was redeemed. Gnosticism is generally considered a Christian heresy. Recent scholarship, however, has indicated that there also existed a pagan Gnosticism. The *Corpus Hermeticum* written by different writers in the 2nd-3rd centuries c.e. is of a pagan gnostic nature, and some of the recently discovered documents found in Nag Hammadi, Egypt, indicate a non-Christian Jewish Gnosticism. Gnosticism posed a major threat to Christianity for three centuries, but it also served to unify and institutionalize it. It was to combat the gnostic beliefs that brought about the episcopal organization of the Christian Church and the formation and development of the New Testament canon.

The Hellenistic-Roman age was a religious age, with a tendency toward monotheism and a common longing for salvation. Old and new cults and religious philosophies sought to solve the problem of human destiny and to present to mankind a means of salvation through knowledge and the understanding of the origin and nature of the universe and of mankind. Near the end of the late 2nd–beginning of the 3rd century c.e., four religious thought systems were prominent and vied for power: Mithraism, Hellenistic Judaism, Gnosticism, and Christianity. Of these, Judaism and Christianity survived and flourished.

This study examines the rise of the Hellenistic-Roman world and its beliefs, revealing parallels found in the modern era concerning socio-political systems, advances in learning, and encounters with previously inaccessible cultures and new religious movements. It explores the religions of the Hellenistic-Roman age, Mithraism, Hellenistic Judaism, Christianity, and Gnosticism, their socio-psychological and historical development, patterns of thought, influence, and their success or failure. It includes a study of the principal mystery cults, Demeter in Eleusis, Dionysus, Isis, and Cybele or Magna Mater, and the philosophies of Stoicism, Epicureanism, and Middle Platonism.

Chapter I

THE HELLENISTIC-ROMAN WORLD

A. Historical Survey

In 359 B.C.E., Philip II became ruler of the kingdom of Macedon, and over the next 20 years engaged in warfare with the independent Greek city-states. By 338, he had subdued virtually the entire Greek peninsula and imposed his rule on most of its city-states. He then turned his attention to the conquest of the vast Persian Empire. Philip, however, did not live to carry out this plan. He was assassinated in 336 as he was about to inaugurate a major festival in the Macedonian capital of Aegae. He was succeeded by his son Alexander III, who inherited not only his father's throne but also his plans for the invasion of Persia.

In the spring of 334, Alexander, barely 22 years old, crossed the Hellespont into Asia Minor and began one of the most successful military campaigns in history. By 331 he had defeated the Persian Darius III at Gaugamela and proceeded eastward through central Asia to Punjab, where in 326 he subdued the Indian king Porus. Alexander was prevented from advancing further when his troops refused to continue. He returned with his army to Babylon where he died in 323 at the age of 33. At the time of his death, he left a vast land empire stretching from the Aegean eastward to the Indus River in India and from the northern shores of the Black Sea south to Nubia and the Sahara in northern Africa.[1]

1. Scholars in general maintain that Alexander was not motivated solely by the desire for territory and military power, but also by the goal of establishing a common world, a universal empire unified by the Greek language and culture. Recent research, however, attempts

Alexander's conquests transformed the geographic dimensions of the Greek world, brought it into close association with oriental traditions and beliefs, and altered the patterns by which the people of the Mediterranean and Near East lived their lives. Large numbers of Greeks from every environment and social class emigrated to the new settlements formed by Alexander's conquests. These immigrants, although the minority, formed the ruling class; they held the majority of the top-level military and political offices. As the conquerors and rulers of the new world, their Greek civilization and language prevailed. It was not, however, the civilization of Classical Greece, but one shaped and adapted to the new environment. This new culture came to be known as "Hellenistic."[2] The language was a form of Greek known as the *koine*, the "common" language that became the *lingua franca*. Knowledge of Greek was essential for advancement in government, business, the military, and for social advancement. A common language and culture facilitated travel among the various parts of the Hellenistic world, and this ease of travel also helped to promote the common civilization throughout the inhabited world. The most diverse populations of the Mediterranean and Near East embraced the new culture. Even the Jewish people, who had always resisted external influences, were not immune from hellenization. The Hellenistic world formed an *oikoumene*, a world community united by a common language and culture.

It is difficult to establish exact limits to the Hellenistic age. Historically, the term is used to refer to the period of history from 331 when Alexander of Macedon defeated the Persian Darius up to Octavius's defeat of Antony and Cleopatra at Actium in 31. Although politically the Hellenistic world came to an end in 31-30 B.C.E., the Hellenistic age cannot be limited to the same period. Hellenistic language and culture continued to flourish under Roman political domination to the extent that it has often been said that "captive Greece captivated her conqueror." Hellenism was effective throughout

---

to prove otherwise, that Alexander's motives were less idealistic and more immediate and practical, and that they were based on the pursuit of personal glory. See, in particular, Peter Green, *Alexander of Macedonia, 356-323 B.C.: A Historical Biography* (Berkeley: University of California, 1991), esp. ch. 10 and nn.

2. The term "Hellenistic" was first used in the 19th century C.E. to designate the Greek civilization that developed and flourished as a result of the conquests of Alexander the Great: a civilization that evolved from that of Classical Greece, but formed its own unique characteristics.

the Roman imperial and early Byzantine periods. Influences of Hellenistic culture are evident up to the Renaissance period. In the study of the development and influence of Hellenistic religions, however, the period ends in the 4th century C.E. and the emergence of the Christian state, which inaugurated a new religious jurisdiction.[3] This study will use the term "Hellenistic" to designate the period from 331 B.C.E., the inauguration of Alexander's empire, to 31 B.C.E., Octavius's victory at Actium. It will use the term "Hellenistic-Roman" for the period from 30 B.C.E. to the 4th century C.E. and the emergence of the Christian world.

The contact of Greek and non-Greek peoples and cultures gradually produced a "syncretism," a mixture of Greek and oriental elements, especially in the realm of religion. Syncretism is considered the main characteristic of the Hellenistic period.[4] At first Greeks and non-Greeks lived in close proximity, each with their own deities and religious traditions. Greek gods were brought to the east by Greek immigrants to serve as local deities of a city or a people, and Eastern gods were brought to the West by slaves, merchants, and mercenaries. This transplantation of deities occurred as early as the 5th and early 4th centuries B.C.E. During the Hellenistic period, the ease of travel and communication encouraged the various cults and religions to expand throughout the known world. Almost every religion in this period was found both in its homeland and in every major center. As they migrated, they became more cosmopolitan. Many took on a new form as they adapted to their new environment. Often they were identified and their legends combined with the national deity of the locality. As the oriental religions became hellenized, their myths and legends were translated into Greek. Although the rites and cultic practices of their deities were usually preserved, they were reinterpreted, often allegorically, to make them suitable to the common Hellenistic ideals and the needs of the community. The reinterpretation of the ancient religious practices sometimes resulted in the creation of a new form of an archaic deity or a new religious movement.

At first, many of these religions were agricultural cults attached to a specific geographical area and people. Their rites were a celebration of the

---

3. Luther H. Martin, *Hellenistic Religions* (New York: Oxford University Press, 1987), 6.

4. Frederick C. Grant, *Hellenistic Religions: The Age of Syncretism* (New York: Liberal Arts, 1953), XIII. See also Helmut Koester, *Introduction to the New Testament* (Philadelphia: Fortress, 1982) 1:164ff.

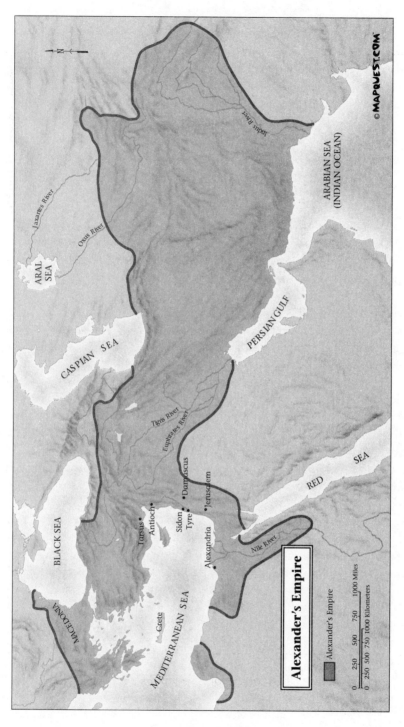

Map 1.1   Alexander's Empire (4th century B.C.E.)

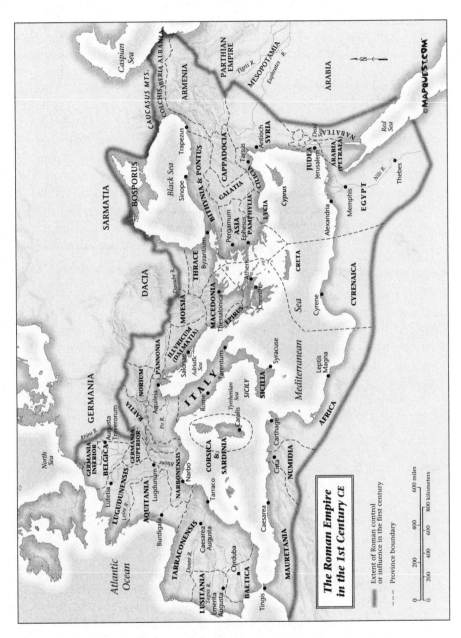

Map 1.2   Roman Empire (1st-2nd centuries c.e.)

seasonal drama of the land. In their native environment, they retained their traditional strength and character with relatively little change. In fact, during this time, many of these native religions restored ancient temples and revived ancient traditional lore in an attempt to re-establish earlier forms and rituals. Outside of their homeland, however, the agricultural rite was equated to the concept of personal salvation, the destiny and salvation of the individual in this life and after death. This interpretation was a response to the changes in individual attitudes and to the new social conditions. As individuals settled outside of their homeland they became estranged from the traditions of their native locale and its particular religion. They no longer considered themselves part of a certain city or town but as a member of the inhabited or known world. As such, they were no longer concerned with the fortunes and destiny of a specific land and its deity, but were interested in a personal god, one with whom they could have a more intimate relationship.

The Greeks had begun to lose confidence in their gods as early as the 5th century. It began with the skepticism of the Sophists about the existence of the Olympian gods and most accepted beliefs about them. In the 4th century, Plato, although not rejecting the existence of the gods, and for political reasons stressing the importance of their worship, understood them as philosophical abstractions rather than anthropomorphic beings. Closely associated with the skepticism of the gods was the development of a new, more expansive view of the world, of mankind and human destiny than that held by the ancient Greek and Near Eastern civilizations. The classical cosmos consisted of a three-tier hierarchy, its summit the vaulted sky on which the stars were scattered, and which the Greeks believed was the dwelling of the gods who controlled all human affairs and events. Beneath the sky was the earth, viewed as a flat disk surrounded by the ocean, and below the earth the underworld where the dead lived as pale shadows.

By the 4th century, the advancement of the science of astronomy produced a concept of the world as an eternal perfect sphere composed of a system of concentric moving spheres. In the center was the earth, the first and oldest of the spheres, suspended in space around which revolved the seven planets. The cosmos was viewed as divided into two realms, a translunar and sublunar, with the moon as the boundary. Above the moon was the sphere of the heavenly bodies, the stars and the planets that move in an eternal harmony. Below it existed the sublunar world, the material world, the place of chance, corruption, mutability, and death.[5] Both the material and spiritual world, the whole universe, was believed to be the creation of a *demiurge,* or creator god. Mankind was believed to be an alien wanderer in the material world. A person's true being, the soul, is immortal and belongs to the spiritual transcendent world. Thus, an individual's aim in life should be to purify himself from the material things of the world and return to fellowship with the divine by cultivating his reason and living a virtuous life in obedience to his divine reason. The rewards and punishments of the soul in the next world depended on the degree to which an individual lived in accordance with his reason in this life.[6]

This new cosmology and view of the individual, together with the new Hellenistic cosmopolitanism, lessened the individual's interest and confidence in the traditional gods and their cults, who were bound to a particular place and its politics. They continued to receive impressive ceremonial worship in the conviction that what was traditional should be preserved. Gifts were offered to the temples, there were numerous votive offerings, processions, and sacrifices, and many festivals and games were reorganized. There was also renewed activity in the building of temples and in temple reforms. However, the ordinary man and woman no longer placed their hope or faith on the ancient gods, whom they believed could not alleviate their daily encounters with the vicissitudes of Hellenistic life. The same was true of the ruler cult that existed both in the Hellenistic and Hellenistic-Roman periods, and which had been established to replace the traditional city-gods in whom the populace had lost confidence. Although the ruler/emperor was considered a *soter,* a "savior," the one who secured and preserved peace and prosperity for his subjects, the cult primarily had political implications. It did not fulfill the needs of the individual man and woman. People searched for a personal savior, one who would offer them strength and support to cope with the changing world in which they lived and immortality and happiness after death. This they found in the cults

5. This world view can be found in the works of Plato (427-348), in the *Laws* and especially in the *Timaeus,* and in the *Metaphysics* and *Meteorology* of Aristotle (384-322). For a discussion of the new worldview and its general religious influence, see Martin P. Nilsson, "The New Conception of the Universe in Late Greek Paganism," *Eranos* 44 (1946): 20-27.

6. The doctrine of rewards and punishments in the next life is stressed in Plato's *Phaedrus* and *Phaedo.*

and their deities that had increasingly penetrated the Greek world during this time, and had become hellenized and transformed from national deities to universal savior divinities. These transformed cults were known as "mysteries," i.e., initiation ceremonies through which individuals were granted admission into fellowship with the divine.[7] With their purification rites, their enthusiasm and ecstasy, and their rewards of immortality through personal identification with the deity, the cults satisfied some spiritual need of the individual, either for salvation, revelation, peace of mind, or inner illumination. To the degree that they met the needs of the time, both the oriental cults and those of the old gods of Greece developed, spread throughout the empire, and enjoyed great appeal, especially during the imperial period.

The term "savior" means deliverer, preserver, protector from all ills, healer, or guide. In the Greek and Hellenistic-Roman world the title was given to individuals, divine or human, male or female, who had improved a situation or had prevented a perilous one, either personal, political, social, or intellectual. These saviors included gods of Classical Greece, mystery cult deities, rulers, Roman emperors, and even philosophers. Salvation, *soteria*, meant deliverance or protection from the vicissitudes of this life, and a better life for the soul after death. Neither the term "salvation" nor any other related word had any theological implications.

B. The Mystery Cults

The mystery cults of the Hellenistic-Roman world were a product of the age, a response to the changing attitudes of individual and social conditions. Both the oriental cults that had penetrated the Greek world and the old Greek cults were hellenized into mystery cults, mysteries, or *mysteria*, a Greek term that meant "initiation." The term was applied to the cults in which membership depended upon the participation of the initiate in a personal ritual that resulted in the individual's identification or close relationship with the deity of the cult. Although secrecy of the initiation rite was a necessary characteristic of these cults, the term "mysteries" (in the plural) was not used to denote something secret or silent. This usage is known primarily from Biblical Greek. It is found in the Septuagint, the let-

---

7. The term "mystery" is explained in greater detail in the section on the mystery cults.

ters of Paul, and in Mark 4:11, and has no relation to the pagan initiation ceremonies.[8]

There were many mystery cults with diverse rites and religious concepts of the mysteries. Nonetheless, three essential characteristics are common to all the mystery cults of the time: (1) a purification rite by which the initiate is granted admission and participation in the activity of the cult; (2) a sense of a personal relationship or communion with the deity or deities of the cult; and (3) the hope or promise of a life of blessedness after death. Four of the more prominent and influential Hellenistic-Roman cults were the cult of Demeter at Eleusis and those of Dionysus, Isis, and Cybele or Magna Mater.

Demeter at Eleusis

The oldest and most significant for the development of the Hellenistic-Roman mysteries was the cult of Demeter situated at Eleusis, some 14 miles west of the city of Athens. Information about the cult is derived from archaeological and literary evidence, the 15th-century Parian Chronicle, and the Homeric *Hymn to Demeter*. The latter is dated to the 7th century, but relates events that occurred long before its composition, and is considered the authoritative account of the Eleusinian tradition.[9]

According to legend, Demeter was the goddess of grain and, along with her daughter Persephone, also known as Kore, was considered a member of the divine Olympian family of gods. One day, while Persephone was picking flowers in a meadow, the earth opened up and Pluto, god of the underworld, sprang forth and carried her away to his kingdom. Stricken with grief, Demeter wandered over the earth for nine days with burning torches, searching for her daughter and refusing to eat. On the 10th day she learned from Helios the truth about her daughter's disappear-

8. Jonathan Z. Smith, *Drudgery Divine: On the Comparison of Early Christianities and the Religions of Late Antiquity* (Chicago: University of Chicago Press, 1990), 60-81; see also A. D. Nock, *Early Gentile Christianity and its Hellenistic Background* (New York: Harper & Row, 1964), 116-24.

9. A discussion of the archaeological and literary evidence of the establishment and development of the cult at Eleusis is found in George E. Mylonas, *Eleusis and the Eleusinian Mysteries* (Princeton: Princeton University Press, 1961), ch. I; see also Martin P. Nilsson, *Greek Folk Religion* (New York: Harper, 1961), 42-64.

ance and that Zeus had consented to the deed. Angered at Zeus, she left Olympus and the gathering of the gods, and, disguised as an old woman, she roamed the countryside and towns looking for Persephone. Finally, she came to Eleusis and was discovered sitting by the Parthenion well by the daughters of Celeus, the ruler of Eleusis. They invited her to the palace where she was offered a drink of wine. She refused the wine but ordered a *kykeon,* a drink of water mixed with barley meal and mint, and with this she broke her fast.

While in Celeus's house, Demeter was nursemaid to Demophon, the royal couple's baby son. During the day, she cared for him as a god and anointed him with ambrosia; but at night, unknown to his parents, she put him in the fire to burn away his mortality. Wondering about her son's amazing growth, Queen Metaniera spied on Demeter and witnessed her in the act. She confronted the goddess, who angrily disclosed her true identity, and ordered that a temple and altar be built to her outside the city walls. When the temple was completed, Demeter sat inside, grieving for her daughter, and caused a great famine that threatened the existence of mankind. Nothing grew throughout the whole earth, and Demeter vowed that nothing would grow until she saw her daughter. Finally, Zeus was compelled to intervene and ordered Pluto to return Persephone to her mother. Before she left the underworld, Pluto gave her a sweet pomegranate seed to eat, thus assuring that she would return. Persephone was obligated to spend four months each year in the underworld with her husband Pluto, but was free to spend the remaining eight months with her mother and the other gods on Olympus. With the return of Persephone to her, Demeter restored vegetation to all the earth, and, before reuniting with her Olympian family, she taught the rulers of Eleusis her rites and all her mysteries, "mysteries which no one may transgress or reveal because a great reverence of the gods restrains utterance."[10]

Traditional evidence places the introduction of the cult of Demeter at Eleusis sometime in the second half of the 15th century.[11] Originally it was a local agrarian family cult, not open to the general public, but limited to those chosen by the head of the family or clan. These included citizens, strangers, and slaves from both sexes and all ages, but only Greeks. Because

10. N. J. Richardson, ed., *The Homeric Hymn to Demeter* (Oxford: Clarendon, 1974), ll. 478-79. The summary of the myth is from the same text.
11. Mylonas, 14, 41.

of the secrecy imposed on the initiates, the cult came to be known as the mysteries of Demeter and, since it was located at Eleusis, the Eleusinian mysteries. Demeter was one of the most important of the Greek deities, deeply rooted in the religious beliefs of the people. Her cult soon spread throughout the Greek world. Sanctuaries were built to her and festivals were performed in her honor. In the 7th century, when Eleusis was annexed to Athens, the cult of Demeter developed into a national institution and created within Greece a society united by a feeling of brotherhood. During the Hellenistic-Roman period, it acquired world-wide significance. Although Demeter was known and celebrated throughout the Greek world, her mysteries were performed only at Eleusis, since it was there that Demeter's wandering had come to an end, and only at the established time.

Initially, the Eleusinian mysteries were concerned with the cultivation of grain and the well-being of the independent community of Eleusis. The festivals were linked to the important stages in the grain cultivation, the plowing and sowing in autumn and the growth of the crops in spring and early summer, and paralleled Persephone's time spent with her mother Demeter and with Pluto. According to the Hymn, her absence in the underworld corresponds to the winter months when the grain is under the ground, and her return, to the spring when the grain is growing as well as other crops and plants.[12] The purpose of the rites that were held in the spring and fall was to promote or sanctify the growth of the crops. It was a time of great joy and happiness, a celebration of the new crop.

By the 7th century, although the celebration of the mysteries retained its relation to the annual cycle of the grain, the mysteries had assumed a different aspect. Demeter not only had power over the fertility of the soil but also over the human soul. This development is reflected in the *Homeric Hymn to Demeter*, believed to have been written sometime in the early 7th century. The mysteries promised prosperity in this life and a blessed immortality to those who had been initiated in the holy rite.[13] By the Hellenistic-Roman period, participation in the mysteries was understood as a personal religious experience that had the power to bestow happiness on

---

12. Richardson, ll. 399-401, 453ff., 471ff.: see also 13ff. A variety of recent interpretations exist concerning the ritual and its significance, but there is no evidence for these understandings; see 284ff.

13. Richardson, ll. 480-90.

an individual and assistance through this life and after death. Beginning in the 7th century, Eleusis acquired immense prestige as a holy place and a shrine of pilgrimage. Individuals from all over the known world sought initiation into the mysteries. The cult's ever-increasing popularity resulted in the continuous expansion and development of the sanctuary and its facilities. It reached the zenith of its development during the Roman imperial period.

The secret or central rites of the Eleusinian mysteries are among the best kept secrets of history. The requirement of silence imposed upon the initiates was very strictly enforced and maintained. Testimonies about the secret rites come from Christian polemic writings and are not reliable. Although knowledge about the secret aspects of the cult is scant, some general information about the cult and its public worship can be gleaned from literary references and works of art dating from the 7th century B.C.E. to the early 3rd century C.E. According to these sources, there were two stages to the Eleusinian mysteries. The first part, known as the Lesser Mysteries, was celebrated in Athens in the early spring and was open to the public. Both those seeking initiation and the general public were permitted to observe and hear all that was said and done. This part of the mysteries included fasting, the ritual of washing and purification by water, and public sacrifice. It served as a preliminary exercise to determine the worthiness of the participants and to prepare them for initiation into the Greater Mysteries, the second and highest stage of the mysteries.

Celebration of the Greater Mysteries was held at Eleusis in late September and lasted for 10 days, the length of time that Demeter spent searching for her daughter before she learned the truth of her disappearance. Many and varied ceremonies were conducted during this time in preparation for the final initiation, which took place in the temple known as the Telesterion. As in the Lesser Mysteries, the initiates participated in a cleansing and purification ritual, sacrifices, prayers, fasting, and the drinking of the *kykeon*, by which they, like Demeter, broke their fast.[14] Each initiate was under the direction of a sponsor, presumably a member of one of the two leading families of Athens, who served as an administrative functionary of the celebration. The religious aspects of the festival were conducted by the priesthood of Eleusis and included six different offices. Every initiate paid various religious functionaries an *obol* (equal to a

14. For a discussion of each day's activities, see Mylonas, 243-80.

sixth of a drachma) a day for their services. Total cost for initiation, including the Lesser Mysteries, was 15 drachmae.[15] The final ritual of the ceremony included three elements: the *dromena,* the things demonstrated; the *legomena,* the words spoken; and the *deiknoumena,* the objects that were shown. Although it is not known for certain what was done, said, and shown, evidence from later sources indicates that part of the *dromena* included a sacred pageant, a re-enactment of the abduction of Persephone, Demeter's wandering, and their reunion at Eleusis. No evidence or information exists about the *legomena,* the words spoken, or the *deiknoumena,* the sacred objects shown. Scholars, however, believe that the *legomena* were brief statements and explanations of the *dromena.* The sacred objects shown were the most important and most secret. Their disclosure would have been severely punished; thus the secret was faithfully maintained.

Although the full content and meaning of the Eleusinian mysteries was and still is unknown, the rites of Eleusis continued to be held for 2000 years and to satisfy the deepest longings and most sincere yearnings of humanity. Cicero succinctly described them when, after his initiation, he stated that Athens has given nothing more excellent or divine to the world than the Eleusinian mysteries: "we recognize in them the true principles of life" and have learned from them "how to live in happiness and how to die with a better hope."[16] The immense prestige and popularity of Eleusis influenced other Greek cults and the development of the Hellenistic-Roman mysteries. During the Hellenistic-Roman period, the cult attracted large crowds from all parts of the known world and many, including several emperors, were initiated into the mysteries. However, not everyone who sought initiation was accepted, only people of approved moral character. Nero never visited Eleusis because he knew that he would probably be denied initiation, and Appollonius of Tyana was refused participation because he was considered a magician.[17]

---

15. Mylonas, 229-37.
16. Cicero *Leg.* 2.36-38.
17. Mylonas, 155, 248.

Dionysus

The cult of Dionysus, known by the Romans as Bacchus, was the most widely spread and the most popular, after that of Demeter. Dionysus was worshipped everywhere, from the Black Sea to Egypt and from Asia Minor to southern Italy. In contrast to the cult of Demeter, his was never institutionalized and there was no specific location for the performance of the rites as were those of Eleusis. The lack of a centralized organization has resulted in many varying accounts of the god, his birth, and his adventures, most of which are inconsistent with one another. Evidences exist of the great diffusion and diversity in the worship and cults of Dionysus, which reveal many and different origins.[18]

Dionysus's true origin is obscure. Many theories exist, but the meager evidences seem to indicate that he originated somewhere in Asia Minor and was incorporated into the Greek tradition as early as the late 2nd millennium B.C.E. He is mentioned in the Mycenaean Linear B tablets of the 12th century and in the works of Homer.[19] In the traditional and most familiar version of the myth, Dionysus was the son of the god Zeus and a mortal woman, Semele, one of the four daughters of Cadmus, king of Thebes. Before she could give birth to him, Semele was consumed by fire when she momentarily glimpsed Zeus's divine brilliance. Zeus immediately snatched the unborn child from the fire and concealed him in his thigh until the time of his birth. This gave Dionysus a mortal and divine nature. Like Demeter, Dionysus was originally a god of nature, the life-giving force of all growing things, animal and vegetable. Eventually, he was regarded as the god of the vine and was associated with the festivals of viticulture, the cultivation of grapes, held in the early spring and fall. The spring festival was a celebration of the pruning of the vines, the one in the fall when the grapes were harvested. Initially, only women participated in the celebrations.

It is difficult to trace the development of Dionysus's rites because he was understood differently from place to place and the cultic practices were varied. Nonetheless, it is evident from descriptions in literature and through numerous works of art that by the 5th century the cult was very popular and many of its rites were celebrated publicly. A well-known de-

18. A summary of the various theories concerning the origin of Dionysus's cult is found in Walter F. Otto, *Dionysus, Myth and Cult* (Bloomington: Indiana University Press, 1965), ch. 2.

19. Walter Burkert, *Greek Religion* (Cambridge, Mass.: Harvard University Press, 1985), 53-58.

scription of the public rites during the Classical period is found in the choral songs of the *Bacchae* of Euripides (ca. 480-406). There is also evidence of the existence of private initiation rites practiced by small local or family groups.[20] By then, the seasonal ceremonies of the renewal of plant and animal life were regarded as the symbol of an individual's own eternal destiny. During this time, the Dionysiac *orgia,* a Greek term meaning "sacred rites," were concerned with the blessed life of the initiates in the afterlife. Participation in the rites of Dionysus provided one with a special knowledge that led to a blessed and divine state. The final achievement of this blessed state was realized in the underworld.[21]

A development of the cult of Dionysus during the Classical period was the theater and the two dramatic forms, tragedy and comedy, which served as a principal expression of the public worship of Dionysus and were an essential part of Greek culture. "Tragedy" *(tragodia)* is derived from two Greek words meaning "song of the goat." It was so called because a goat was sacrificed to Dionysus before the choral hymn was sung. At first, the subject of tragedy was concerned with the story of Dionysus and belonged to the spring festival held in March. It was later extended to include the stories of heroes, especially those found in the works of Homer. "Comedy" *(komodia)* means "song of the revellers," a group of villagers who honored the god of wine with dancing and singing. Comedy was a part of the winter festival of Dionysus. Its purpose was to celebrate the new wine and to cheer the people during the long dreary winter months.[22]

Dionysus enjoyed great popularity in the ancient Greek world, but it was not until the Hellenistic-Roman age that his cult gained wide acceptance and was publicly promoted by kings and emperors. Next to the god of healing, Asclepius, Dionysus was the most revered. His popularity was due not only to the fact that the initiate into his mysteries acquired a new status, as did the initiates in the Demeter rites, but he was also made a member of a group of like-minded individuals who spoke the same language and had a similar hope for the hereafter.[23]

20. Susan Guettel Cole, "New Evidence for the Mysteries of Dionysos," *GRBS* 21 (1980): 236-37.

21. Cole, 231-34.

22. For a discussion of the origin of tragedy and comedy, see C. Kerényi, *Dionysos: Archetypal Image of Indestructible Life.* Bollingen Series 65, vol. 2 (Princeton: Princeton University Press, 1976), 315-48.

23. Nock, 115.

By the 3rd century B.C.E., the Dionysiac cult was widespread in Egypt and Asia Minor and favored by their kings, many of whom considered themselves descendants of the god. Although scant information exists about the rites and concepts of the Dionysiac mysteries in Egypt, there is sufficient evidence to indicate their importance. During his reign, Ptolemy II Philadelphus (282-246) instituted a magnificent procession in which a statue of Dionysus was the central figure. It was accompanied by a large entourage of the god's followers and surrounded by most of the paraphernalia of his cults and mysteries.[24] Ptolemy IV Philopater (222-204) claimed to be a descendant of Dionysus and had the ivy leaf of the god tattooed on his body. An edict of the king preserved on papyrus and dating from ca. 210 orders all initiation priests of Dionysus to register in Alexandria and to declare from whom they had received the holy rites, up to three generations. They then had to turn over to a royal official the sacred book, sealed and inscribed with their name.[25] The purpose of the edict is uncertain, but it is evidence of the cult's popularity and the king's interest in it. Similarly, the kings of the Attalid kingdom of Pergamum in Asia Minor claimed Dionysus as their ancestor, and he was worshipped as the official god of the realm.

During this time, Italy also witnessed a surge of Dionysiac popularity. Archaeological findings reveal that Dionysus or Bacchus, as he was called by the Romans, was known and popular in Italy as early as the 6th century. Evidence shows that the Bacchic rites of initiation were a form of private, not public, worship and were often performed informally by small local or family organizations. The emphasis of the ceremonies was preparation for an afterlife of punishments and/or bliss.[26] By the end of the 3rd or early 2nd century, the cult had taken on the fervor of a religious missionary movement. The initiates held secret meetings and had secret signs by which they recognized each other, and changes were made to the initiation ceremonies, or Bacchanalia. Wine-drinking and feasting were added to the religious component, which led to ecstatic fanaticism and the practice of scandalous behavior. At first, the rites were imparted to a few, but soon they were propagated widely in order to gain many adherents. The move-

24. Martin P. Nilsson, *The Dionysiac Mysteries of the Hellenistic and Roman Age* (New York: Arno, 1975), 11.

25. The decree is quoted in H. Idris Bell, *Cults and Creeds in Graeco-Roman Egypt* (New York: Philosophical Library, 1953), 18.

26. Cole, 235-37.

ment caused great consternation throughout Italy. Their numbers had reached such proportions that they were considered almost a second state. In 186, the Roman senate considered them a seditious group and a genuine threat to the public security and passed legislation to suppress them.

[handwritten: 18ure?] The senate's decree, the *Senatus Consultum de Bacchanalibus,* prohibited the Bacchanalia and all other cults that held secret meetings. Because Bacchus was an acknowledged member of the pantheon, the public cult could not be forbidden completely, but it too was severely restricted. No more than two men and three women could be present at a rites ceremony, and the group was forbidden to have a common treasury or cult officials. This restriction was to prevent the Bacchanalia from operating under the guise of a public cult.[27]

Although suppressed, the movement did not disappear completely. A small remnant remained underground and resurfaced and grew sometime in the late 1st century B.C.E. to early 1st century C.E. A 2nd-century C.E. inscription from Tusculum provides a membership list of 500 names arranged according to their religious rank. Other inscriptions from the imperial period suggest that the movement enjoyed its greatest popularity during the 2nd and 3rd centuries C.E. This movement lacked the religious fervor of the original group, and its mysteries were free from fanaticism. The new Bacchic mysteries were especially favored by the affluent population, who celebrated the rites in their homes and decorated their houses with detailed representations of them. It is the frescoes and mosaics found in these homes and villas that provide the existing information about the Bacchic mysteries in Italy.[28]

Bacchus's popularity continued through the 4th century C.E., as attested by the literature and iconography of the period. During this time, he was considered the god of wine and of joy. It is this aspect of the god that appealed to many of the affluent of Italy. The Bacchic mysteries that were celebrated in their homes consisted mostly of great feasting and rejoicing, to which was added a small part of the religious ceremony.[29]

---

27. An account of the Bacchanalia and the Senate's decree are found in the works of the Roman historian Livy (59 B.C.E.–17 C.E.), 39:8-19. The narrative is summarized and discussed in Nilsson, *Dionysiac Mysteries,* 14-21.

28. For a description and discussion of the art works, see Nilsson, *Dionysiac Mysteries,* 66-115.

29. Nilsson, *Dionysiac Mysteries,* 74, 146.

[handwritten: senate said they needed to do away with Dionysics]

Isis

Of all the Hellenistic cults, that of Isis is considered the most beautiful and gentle and in some ways the most important of the mystery cults. In her native Egypt, Isis was, from time immemorial, the goddess of life and was identified with every living being. Little is known of the origins of Isis or her character. It seems that she existed independently as a cosmic deity, the embodiment of the Nile's annual reawakening that was so essential for the livelihood of the Egyptians.[30] In the *Pyramid Texts,* the oldest body of Egyptian religious texts, written in the 3rd millennium B.C.E., Isis is represented with her son Horus and Osiris, the god of vegetation and death, as a family unity in a series of unconnected allusions to the myth that developed and was later known in the Hellenistic world.[31]

The *Pyramid Texts* represent Isis as the goddess of the earth and of fertility. Osiris was identified with the stagnant Nile, which was reborn yearly as the living water Horus that rose to inundate the land and restore it to new life. Throughout Egyptian history, the pharaohs were the human embodiment of the youthful Horus and thus the son of Isis, the Goddess Mother and ruler of the living. At death, the pharaohs were identified with Osiris, the god of the dead and of its kingdom.[32] Many disconnected versions and developments of the Isis and Osiris myth are found throughout the ancient Egyptian texts. A complete connected version of the myth is found in Plutarch's treatise *On Isis and Osiris,* written ca. 118-119 C.E., and is a product of the Hellenistic-Roman era.[33]

In its classical form, the myth relates the encounter of Osiris and his twin brother Seth, in which Seth kills Osiris, dismembers his body, and casts the pieces into the Nile, and Isis's subsequent mourning for her brother. Initially, Osiris was considered only as Isis's brother. It was not until the late 3rd millennium that he was also designated as her husband.[34] Mourning, Isis, with her sister Nephtys, searches tirelessly for Osiris's body. Upon finding the pieces of his body, they assembles them and per-

---

30. Sharon Kelly Heyob, *The Cult of Isis Among Women in the Graeco-Roman World.* EPRO 51 (Leiden: E. J. Brill, 1975), 37.

31. Heyob, 38.

32. R. E. Witt, *Isis in the Graeco-Roman World* (Ithaca: Cornell University Press, 1971), 15.

33. Heyob, 38.

34. Heyob, 38.

forms the embalming rites that result in Osiris's resuscitation.[35] In the early tradition of the myth, Osiris was the central figure. Isis was subordinate to him in importance and popularity, and her main duty was to mourn his death and to seek his revival.[36] She was mourner, wife, and mother. It was in her hellenized form that Isis gained the supremacy and developed into a universal deity who was the fulfillment of the deepest emotional needs of the people of that time.

Isis was known to the Greek world as early as the 5th century B.C.E. from the histories of Herodotus (ca. 480-430), in which she is identified with the Eleusinian Demeter.[37] By the mid-4th century, inscriptions of Isis were found in Athens and other parts of Greece, and by the end of the 3rd century her cult had spread widely throughout the Greek world, especially in port cities and centers of commerce, and was familiar to the Roman world as well.[38] Isis's early identification with Demeter facilitated the popularity and expansion of her cult and enhanced her role as wife and mother. Both had wandered, mourned, and suffered for a beloved family member, and both were successful in the restoration of the lost family member.[39] Although Isis acquired new attributes and roles as she spread throughout the Hellenistic-Roman world, her dominant trait was as devoted wife and mother, the divine patroness of family life.[40]

The essential characteristics and roles of the hellenized Isis are found in the aretalogies, a series of Greek hymns that praise and recite her virtues. These are preserved in a number of variant forms dating from the 1st century B.C.E.[41] In the aretalogies, Isis is depicted not as the Egyptian vegetative goddess of the Nile, but as the supreme universal deity, the one and only divinity worshipped by all the world under many different names and in varied forms and rites.[42] She was the "Goddess of Countless Names"

35. Heyob, 38.

36. Heyob, 40.

37. Herodotus *Hist.* 2:59, 156.

38. Heyob, 7-9.

39. Friedrich Solmsen, *Isis among the Greeks and Romans* (Cambridge, Mass.: Harvard University Press, 1979), 24-25.

40. Witt, 41.

41. The oldest extant version of the aretalogies is the 1st-century *Andros Hymn*. A well-known later version is found in the 11th book of Apuleius's *Metamorphoses*, late 2nd century C.E. For a discussion of the various texts of the aretalogies, see Heyob, 45-47 and n. 39.

42. Apul. *Metam.* 11:5.

who, through the process of syncretism, had assimilated within herself both the names and functions of every other divinity, Egyptian and Hellenistic-Roman. Isis was known as mistress of the heavens, the earth, the sea, and even the underworld.[43] More powerful than Fate, she was ruler of the universe, all-powerful and all-seeing. All civilization was her creation and her charge. Isis established laws that can never be broken, and was the lawgiver and the champion of justice. She invented navigation, gave speech to mankind, introduced the art of writing, spinning and weaving, and instructed all people in the cultivation of the land. She gave to mankind all that makes life comfortable and worthwhile. Isis was both protectoress and aide. She gave safety to the sailor struggling on the high seas, protected the wanderer in a foreign land far from home, freed the prisoner, healed those who were sick, and gave comfort to those in distress.[44]

The respective hymns also emphasize her role as the goddess of women and enumerate the reasons why women in particular owed her homage and sought her protection. It was she who brought men and women together, who caused women to be loved by men, who established the marriage contract, ordained that women should bear children, established the parent-child relationship, and was known to punish children who were unkind to their parents and parents who showed no affection. Isis was the patroness and glory of women who gave them equal power with men.[45] In the *Oxyrhynchus Litany,* she is proclaimed the Divine Mother and is identified, among other virtues, with Grace, Beauty, Fortune, Truth, Wisdom, and Love.[46] As the Divine Mother, her maternal care extended to all humanity. Through her own suffering, she understood and sympathized with the sufferings of humanity and embraced all who suffered misfortune in her consoling love. Isis promised to her initiates the fulfillment of their deepest needs, both in this world and in the next.[47] Sculpturally, she was usually portrayed as a young matron in modest dress with gentle, benevolent features, holding the child Horus in her arms. There is artistic evidence, although not conclusive, that the Christian Madonna and Child is patterned after the Isis/Horus iconogra-

43. Apul. *Metam.* 11:5.
44. Witt, ch. VIII.
45. Heyob, 48-52.
46. Bernard P. Grenfell and Arthur S. Hunt, eds., *The Oxyrhynchus Papyri* XI (London: Egypt Exploration Society, 1915): 1380.
47. Apul. *Metam.* 11:6.

phy.[48] Belief in Isis as the only one, true, and living god whose divinity encompassed all other divinities reveals the strong tendency of the time towards universality and monotheism. It also influenced the feminization of the godhead, a concept that was very prevalent during the Hellenistic period. This concept even challenged the strong patriarchal tradition of Hellenistic Judaism.[49]

By the middle of the 2nd century B.C.E., the cult of Isis had become universal and had spread throughout the Hellenistic-Roman world. The mysteries of the cult were a Hellenistic development patterned after those of the Eleusinian Demeter. Information concerning the mysteries is scant, with the exception of Apuleius's *Metamorphoses,* also known as *The Golden Ass;* this material gives only a number of details, but not what actually took place in the sanctuary during the initiation. Although basically a work of fiction, the *Metamorphoses* does contain certain facts. In particular, Book XI provides the most information available on the Isaic initiation and the only full account of an individual's religious experience by an adherent of ancient paganism. Numerous inscriptions and other fragmentary evidences show that this information is more factual than fictive.

According to Apuleius, initiation into the Isaic cult was limited to individuals who were selected by Isis herself and who were able to afford the high expenses involved in the initiation.[50] These individuals were notified of the honor by Isis in a dream. Prior to the initiation, the individual underwent a bath of purification and 10 days of strict fasting. The initiate was then dressed in a linen robe and permitted to enter the sanctuary where he/she wandered in the dark places of the underworld and underwent certain trials.[51] The morning after the initiation, the initiate, standing on a wooden podium before the statue of Isis, was presented to the crowd. This day was considered a new birthday for the initiate. It signified that he/she had died to the old life and was reborn to a new course of life and salvation under the protection of Isis. This protection continued even after death, as long as the initiate remained faithful to her.[52]

Isaic shrines or temples were found throughout the Hellenistic-Roman world, and public services, prayers, and offerings were presented to

48. Witt, 216ff.; see also Solmsen, 126 n. 51.
49. See below, Chapter III.
50. Apul. *Metam.* 11:28.
51. Apul. *Metam.* 11:23.
52. Apul. *Metam.* 11:6.

her daily. In addition, two major public festivals were celebrated annually, the Festival of Seeking and Finding, and the Launching of the Isaic Ship. The daily rituals consisted of four services. The first, a public service, was held before dawn when the temples were opened by the priests. At midday, another service was held for private prayer and meditation. Two additional services were held in the late afternoon and in the evening, after which the temples were closed for the night.[53]

The Festival of Seeking and Finding was a six-day ceremony that took place from October 28 until November 3. It represented Osiris's death and Isis's lamentation, her search for his body, and his subsequent revival that was a cause for great public jubilation.[54] The Launching of the Isaic Ship was held on March 5 and celebrated the advent of Spring. It was the first boat of the season and re-established navigation after the stormy winter during which the sea was not navigable.[55] This festival also symbolized the individual's vicissitudes of life until he/she found rest and peace under the protection and in the service of the goddess Isis.[56]

Cybele — Magna Mater

Cybele is often referred to as the Great Mother, the mother of gods, mankind, mountains, and lions. Like Isis, she was an oriental goddess. She was of Anatolian origin, and according to archaeological evidences, her cult can be traced to the Neolithic age. During her prehistoric existence, Cybele was revered as Earth Mother. In the earliest extant representations dating from ca. 6000 B.C.E., she is seated on a rocky throne, a woman of immense proportions. On either side of her throne stands a leopard, and on each leopard's head she rests a heavy hand protectively and triumphantly.[57] Except for the few statuettes and rock reliefs dating from 6000 to 1500, almost nothing is known about the nature and attributes of the goddess and the character of her cult.

53. Witt, 91-92; cf. Apul. *Metam.* 11:20.

54. Witt, 162, 180-181.

55. Apul. *Metam.* 11:5. The description and symbolism of the ceremony are found in Witt, ch. XIII.

56. Apul. *Metam.* 11:15.

57. Maarten J. Vermaseren, *Cybele and Attis: the Myth and the Cult* (London: Thames and Hudson, 1977), 15-16.

Inscriptional and iconographical evidence reveals that sometime during the 12th century Cybele's cult began to spread throughout Asia Minor. As it came into contact with other cultures, it underwent various transformations. In the Phrygian kingdom of Asia Minor, the cult acquired special importance, especially during the reign of King Midas (725-675). The Phrygians regarded Cybele as their national goddess, and she is often called the Phrygian goddess. Cybele became an important part of Phrygian legends, and monuments to her are found throughout the territory, in both early and later times.[58] It was in Phrygian Pessinus that she had her primary sanctuary. In Phrygia, music became a major part of the cult, and the Phrygian rock monuments represent the goddess either standing or enthroned, flanked by two lions, and often accompanied by two small musicians, one playing the double-pipe and the other the lyre. The Phrygians are also responsible for the wild and barbaric features of the cult, the loud ululations and wild dances that incited people to bloody self-flagellation and self-mutilation.

Cybele was adopted by the Greeks who had migrated to Asia Minor early in the 12th century. They eliminated the orgiastic Phrygian elements from the cult and introduced it to Greece and to the western colonies. By the 7th century, Cybele was widely worshipped in Greece, where she was known as *Meter theon*, Mother of the Gods, or *Meter oreie*, Mother of the Mountains. Like Demeter and Isis, Cybele was initially the goddess of the earth and of fertility, and like them came to be regarded as the inventor of agriculture and of legal order. The *Homeric Hymns*, generally ascribed to the 7th century, refer to her as the mother of all gods and all mankind, of all animals and of all life.[59] She is surrounded with howling wolves and roaring lions, and rejoices in the sound of cymbals, drums, and flutes that produce a wild, rousing music.[60] This led to ecstatic frenzy in the celebrants, and in receptive devotees to a state of divine possession. As earth mother, Cybele was closely associated with Demeter, and this facilitated her popularity throughout Greece.

In the Classical period, sanctuaries of Cybele were found everywhere in Greece. Her sanctuary in the Athenian agora served as the depository

---

58. Vermaseren, 19.

59. T. W. Allen and E. E. Sikes, eds. *The Homeric Hymns* (New York: Macmillan, 1904), Hymn 14, 30.

60. Allen and Sikes, Hymn 14.

for the state archives. By the beginning of the 5th century, the cult of Cybele was associated with that of Dionysus. The poets Pindar (518-438)[61] and Euripides (480-406)[62] emphasized the similarities between the rites of the two cults, especially in dance and ecstasy. Common to both were the cymbals, drums, the flute, the ecstatic dance of a procession of men and women, and the coursing over the mountains. During this time, the rites of Cybele held no initiatory elements and esoteric structure typical of the mystery cults. To the ancient Greek world, Cybele was a nature goddess, ruler of an uncultivated world inhabited by beasts and venerated with the sound of sacred instruments. As in other cults, it was not until the Hellenistic-Roman period that her character and rituals acquired a mystery form. Nonetheless, Greece was never very supportive of the cult, and neither its Asiatic features of worship nor her consort Attis ever became popular. That the goddess was worshipped at all was due to her identification with certain of the Greek gods. In the mainland and islands of Greece, the cult seems to have retained its Hellenic form. It is not known to what extent, if any, the new initiatory ceremonies and the *taurobolium* sacrifice were assimilated in the Greek cult during the Hellenistic-Roman period. Cybele's prominence and growth during this time comes primarily from Roman sources.

Cybele was introduced at Rome in 204 B.C.E. when the city was desperately seeking deliverance from the powerful Hannibal. She was the first, and for a long time the only, oriental goddess to be recognized in Rome. Various versions of her arrival exist. The most prevalent is that given by the historian Livy.[63] According to Livy, after Rome had struggled with Hannibal's armies for almost 14 years, the city's *decemviri*, a special commission of 10 men in charge of all foreign worship, decided to consult the prophetic Sibylline Books. The books declared that whenever a foreign power had waged war on Italy, he could only be driven away and conquered if the Great Mother was brought to Rome from Pessinus. A Roman delegation was thus sent to King Attalus at Pergamum, who gave them the idol of the goddess. Cybele arrived in Rome on April 4, 204 B.C.E. At first she was received as a guest in the Temple of Victory on the western slope of the Palatine. The day was declared a holiday and came to be celebrated an-

---

61. Pindar *Pyth. III*, 77ff.; frag. 95, 2.
62. Euripides *Bacch.* 58-59; 72-82.
63. Livy *History of Rome* 10:10-14.

nually with a *lectisternium,* a ceremonial banquet at which her grateful and devoted populace brought gifts; the *Megalensia,* a series of public games; and the *lavatio,* the bathing of the goddess's image in the Almo River. This was a Phrygian feature that was brought to Rome with the goddess. Also in 204, by decree of the senate, a temple was commissioned for her to be built on the summit of the Palatine. It was completed in 191 and dedicated on April 10. It is assumed that it was at this time that the original one-day celebration was extended to seven days, from April 4, the anniversary of Cybele's arrival in Rome, to April 10, the day of the dedication of her temple.[64]

Cybele became an important part of Roman life. She was integrated in the Roman pantheon and was considered the great protectress of the city who had brought peace and plenty. Her cult was generously supported by the government and was under patrician patronage. During the annual procession of the goddess, her priests were permitted to collect money for its support freely by begging from door to door. One of her priests was known to have gained admission to the Roman senate.[65] Nonetheless, the Roman authorities could not accept certain of the Phrygian features of the cult, and from its introduction at Rome restricted Roman participation in it. The extravagance in the ceremonies, the barbaric corybantic enthusiasm of the *galli,* or eunuch priests, their mad hypnotic dances accompanied by the loud shrill of the flute, and the sound of the tympanum that led to their self-mutilation were abhorrent to the Romans. Consequently, except for the processions and public games, the *Megalensia* rites were confined to the precincts of the temple on the Palatine, and popular participation in the cult was forbidden. Romans could not serve as priests, play the sacred instruments, or take part in the orgies. All this changed beginning with the time of Claudius (41-54 C.E.).

During the reign of Claudius, the cult gained new vigor and was one of the most popular and most favored of the foreign cults. By the end of the 1st century C.E., its popularity had spread throughout the Western world and in Asia Minor. The restrictions on Roman participation were removed. Roman citizens, both men and women, took part in the processions and Roman men were permitted into the ranks of the *galli.* In addition, although the *Megalensia* continued to be celebrated in April, a new

64. Grant Showerman, *The Great Mother of the Gods* (Chicago: Argonaut, 1969), 34-35.
65. Showerman, 37-38.

annual cycle of events was established by Claudius. The new festival, which was held March 15-27, introduced Cybele's consort Attis into the Roman cult. It is thought that this festival was the original Phrygian cycle initially ignored by the Romans.[66] From that time on Attis was honored as a divinity together with Cybele. The significance of the rituals performed during the festival is not certain, and many hypotheses exist. The interpretations presented here are those most widely accepted and found in early literary works, artifacts, and inscriptions.[67]

The festival began on the Ides of March, March 15. On this day, a six-year-old bull was sacrificed by the cult's high priest, priestess, and *cannophori*, or reed-bearers, for the purpose of promoting the fertility of the mountain fields. The *cannophori* then carried reeds to the temple of the goddess. This is believed to be a commemoration of the early days of Attis based on an early version of the legend. According to the legend, Attis as a child was abandoned among the reeds by the banks of the Gallus River and was rescued by shepherds who raised him. A nine-day period of fasting and abstinence began on March 16. On March 22, a pine tree was cut, decorated, and carried to the temple, where it lay in state. This represents the pine tree next to which Attis is often depicted and under which it is believed he bled to death following his self-mutilation in service to the goddess. March 23 was a day of fasting and mourning commemorating the death of Attis. The following day, March 24, was the "day of blood," during which the *galli* priests flagellated themselves in a frenzied ecstatic dance and sprinkled the blood on the image of the goddess and the altars, and the novices mutilated themselves and became priests of the cult. This is not considered an initiation rite but a form of sacrifice to the goddess. March 25 was the day of joy, or *hilaria*, and was a commemoration of the triumph of day over night after the spring equinox. In the reign of Antoninus Pius (138-161), this day became one of the main Roman festivals. The day following the *hilaria* was a day of rest, and the festival was concluded on March 27 with the *lavatio*, the ceremonious bathing of Cybele's silver statue in the Almo River. This symbolized the irrigation of the earth, which provides vegetation.

The March rituals, as developed and practiced by the Romans, show no evidence of any mystery rites as found in the mystery cults. Rather, they

---

66. Showerman, 50-51.
67. See esp. Showerman, ch. 4; and Vermaseren, ch. 5 and nn.

are rituals commemorating the annual alternation of the seasons, the withering of the earth's vegetation in the winter and its return in the spring. There is no indication of a dying and rising god, of an initiation or purification rite of the worshippers, participation in the life of the deity, or hope of immortality. A cult initiation rite is not attested until the 4th century C.E.

In the 2nd century C.E., the *taurobolium*, the sacrifice of the bull (or a variant, the *criobolium*, the sacrifice of a ram), was introduced into the cult. The earliest inscription of this rite comes from Puteoli, Italy, and dates to 134, but gives no evidence of the meaning of the act. Inscriptional records dating from 160 to ca. 285 indicate that *taurobolia* were performed throughout the year by priests of Cybele or state priests. They were offered on behalf of the welfare of the empire, the emperor, the senate, the armed forces, or a particular individual.[68] They were not initiation rites, but sacrifices to ward off earthly catastrophes from those on whose behalf they were offered. By the 4th century, the *taurobolium* or the *criobolium* had become a rite of initiation and purification. It was the central rite of the cult and was practiced until its demise.

The principal source for the details of the *taurobolium* as a purification rite is found in the *Peristephanon* of Prudentius,[69] a Latin poet of the late 4th century, which recounts the consecration of a high priest. According to Prudentius, the tattooed[70] priest in ceremonial attire descended into a pit over which a bull was slaughtered and was bathed by the bull's blood. When he re-emerged, he was hailed and honored by the crowd of worshippers as one who was reborn. The purpose of the blood baptism was the spiritual purification of the initiate and his rebirth to a new life. Evidence exists that in the 4th century the *taurobolium* or *criobolium* was also celebrated by individual devotees, if they could afford the price of the necessary bull or ram. The period of rebirth was usually 20 years, after which time it had to be repeated. However, a 376 C.E. altar inscription claims that it was forever.[71] A sacred meal followed the ceremony and included the initiate's affirmation of faith with the words, "I have eaten from the tympanum, I have drunk from the cymbal, I have become an initiate of Attis." It

68. Vermaseren, 105.

69. Prudentius *Peristephanon* 10:1011-50.

70. Prudentius *Peristephanon* 10:1076-85. Devotees of Cybele had to receive a tattoo mark on their body, burned into the skin with hot needles. It was a mark of consecration.

71. Showerman, 63.

is not known what was eaten or drunk. The significance of the event is that the sacred instruments of Cybele and Attis became appropriately the plate and cup of the sacramental meal.

Cybele's rites were primitive, wild, and extreme, and her festivals were filled with frenzied music and dances. Nonetheless, except for Greece, her cult continued to gain great popularity and spread to every part of the known world. Her popularity throughout Asia Minor and the northern and western provinces was as great as it was in Rome. To many, Cybele's severe and rigorous demands provided a deep religious experience and a psychological exhilaration.

The mystery cults enjoyed great success during the Hellenistic-Roman period. This was due to the fact that they were international and universal. With the exception of Mithraism, membership was open to all regardless of sex, nationality, or race. At a time of uncertainty and social fluidity, this feature was especially appealing. They were individualistic, addressing the spiritual needs of the individual, and they also provided the devotees with meaningful fellowship with individuals who possessed the same knowledge of salvation. Last, they provided a personal, closer relationship to the divine, protection from the adversities of this life, and the hope of some sort of blissful world after death. The benefits that the cults provided were also attempted by the religious philosophies of the time.

Social fluidity: a society that can change easily.

C. Religious Philosophies

The philosophies of the Hellenistic-Roman age were above all a way of life based on reason that offered inner security and stability. Although they differed in their method, they all promised their followers the same self-sufficient, imperturbable tranquility that provided protection from the miseries and vicissitudes of life. They were a shelter for the soul and offered peace of mind. A number of important philosophical systems existed during this period, but the most significant are Stoicism, Epicureanism,[72]

72. There are a number of good discussions on Stoicism and Epicureanism, among which are: A. H. Armstrong, *Introduction to Ancient Philosophy* (Boston: Beacon, 1963); Armstrong, ed., *The Cambridge History of Later Greek and Early Medieval Philosophy* (Cambridge: Cambridge University Press, 1967); Benjamin Farrington, *The Faith of Epicurus* (London: Weidenfeld and Nicolson, 1967); A.-J. Festugière, *Epicurus and His Gods* (Oxford: Blackwell, 1955); Robert Drew Hicks, *Stoic and Epicurean* (1910, repr. New York: Russell &

and a revived Platonism known as Middle Platonism.[73] These philosophies had the greatest influence on subsequent philosophical and religious thought. Stoicism and Epicureanism were products of the Hellenistic-Roman world and emerged to meet the needs of the time. The aim of both was the attainment of individual happiness through self-sufficiency, i.e., to liberate oneself from all that is external, and both stressed ethics and morality. Middle Platonism was fundamentally rooted in the teachings of Plato, but also combined elements of Aristotelian logic, Stoic psychology and ethics, and Pythagorean mysticism in different proportions by different philosophers of the time. It arose in the latter part of the 1st century B.C.E. and early 1st century C.E., at a time when the austere ideals of Stoicism and the skepticism of Epicureanism were no longer adequate to satisfy the religious longings of humankind.

Stoicism STOIC - NO emotion

Stoicism was founded in Athens by Zeno (ca. 335-265 B.C.E.), a native of Citium on Cyprus. Its name was derived from the place where Zeno taught, an open colonnade, or *stoa,* in the agora or marketplace of Athens. Stoicism flourished and was the most popular and influential philosophical system from the 3rd century B.C.E. to the early 2nd century C.E. It was both metaphysical and a system of ethics with the primary interest and emphasis on ethics.

The Stoics claimed that the universe is a single ordered whole, a perfect organism that unites within itself all that exists in the world. It is ruled by a supreme cosmic power, a fiery substance that the Stoics called Logos, Divine Reason, or God. The Logos is the organizing, integrating, and energizing principle of the whole universe. As a perfect entity, the universe combines within itself the Logos or Divine Reason, which is its soul, and matter, which serves as its body. Since everything is derived from God, ev-

Russell, 1962); Paul Oskar Kristeller, *Greek Philosophers of the Hellenistic Age* (New York: Columbia University Press, 1993); A. A. Long and D. N. Sedley, eds., *The Hellenistic Philosophers,* 1: *Translations of Principal Sources with Philosophical Commentary* (Cambridge: Cambridge University Press, 1987); F. H. Sandbach, *The Stoics* (New York: Norton, 1975).

73. The discussion on the Middle Platonists is summarized from Antonía Tripolitis, *The Doctrine of the Soul in the Thought of Plotinus and Origen* (Roslyn Heights, N.Y.: Libra, 1978), 24-36 and nn. 42-45.

erything is a part of God, but not separated or cut from the whole. Each individual soul is a fragment of the universal Logos or God. Early Stoicism did not believe in the eternality of the world, but in a successive, endless series of world periods, a recurring cycle of predetermined intervals. At the end of a world period, the cosmos is re-absorbed into the divine Fire through a universal conflagration and is then remade. Every new world is exactly the same in every detail. All people and all events of the past repeatedly return. Everything is determined by an unbreakable chain of cause and effect. Thus the universe is the product of a divine plan under a universal law that is God.

Since the human soul is a part of the Divine Reason or God that pervades, determines, and controls everything in the universe, the Stoics maintained that the principal goal of an individual is the pursuit of virtue. Virtue is living in harmony with one's own nature and the nature of the cosmos, namely God. The virtuous individual is one who has attained inner discipline by controlling all emotions and passions and, if possible, eradicating them completely. Human passions and emotions were considered by the Stoics as irrational reason and are diseases of the soul. Liberated from its affections, the individual arrives at a state of apathy, a state of indifference to pleasure, pain, wealth, poverty, fortune, and misfortune and accepting of all that happens. The world and everything in it are determined by God and thus good. True freedom and happiness are achieved when one accepts what is ordained. Thus, despite the miseries and vicissitudes in the world, an individual could find inner peace and independence.

In the mid-2nd century B.C.E., Stoicism had become gentler and more humane. It abandoned the concept of the conflagration of the world and its subsequent restoration, and accepted the Platonic view of the eternity of the world and humanized its view of the virtuous individual. The emphasis now was on the harmonious balance between the affections of the body and the soul. One of the main tenets of later Stoicism was the idea of universal brotherhood. Since the world is a single perfect organism infused by the Logos or Divine Reason and every individual possesses a fragment of that Reason, then every person is an equal citizen of the world under one universal law that is God and all are children of God and brothers and sisters of each other. Along with the concept of universal brotherhood, the Stoics developed the ideas of duty and responsibility to each other and to the world in general. They encouraged public service, and the philosophy was very popular among political leaders during the Hellenistic-Roman period. Stoicism had a considerable influence on the development of later philosophical and religious thought. In particular, it affected the doctrine of the Logos, the Stoic idea of the Divine Reason as the guide of life, and the concept of universal brotherhood. Affinity to the Stoic Logos is found in the Logos doctrine of Philo of Alexandria, the Gospel of John (1:1-14), and in several passages in the Epistle to the Hebrews (4:12). The Stoic doctrines that one should live in accordance with Divine Reason and that of universal brotherhood were adopted and developed by Christianity.

Epicureanism

The Epicurean school bears the name of its founder Epicurus (341-270 B.C.E.), a contemporary of Zeno. The school was founded in 306 and met in the garden of Epicurus's residence in Athens. It was open to all, male and female, slave and free, people from all walks of life. Similar to Stoicism, the aim of Epicureanism was the attainment of dispassionate inner peace and tranquility, which they called *ataraxia*, invulnerability to all circumstances and changes of fortune. *Ataraxia* is attained by the control of the passions and the elimination of fear. The main fears, according to the Epicureans, are fear of death and the afterlife, a concern also shared by the mystery religions, and fear of the gods. To relieve humanity of these fears and give it peace of mind, the Epicureans espoused an atomic worldview first taught in the 5th century by Democritus of Abdera and Leucippus of Miletus. According to this view, nothing exists except atoms composed of matter and void or space. The world was caused by the atoms swerving and colliding as they fell freely through space. Everything in the world consists of atoms and thus is wholly material, even the human soul. Being material, the soul is mortal and is born and disintegrates with the body. Thus one should not fear death or an afterlife, since death is simply extinction, devoid of all feeling or consciousness.

Epicureanism postulated the existence of gods, but perceived them anthropomorphically; they are composed of atoms and have ethereal bodies. They exist eternally in the calm, empty spaces between the heavenly spheres, remote, in perfect tranquility, an existence of ideal happiness, and neither cause nor are concerned about human affairs or earthly events. To do so would only serve to denigrate their undisturbed tranquility. Therefore, there is no need to fear the gods, to worship them, or to win their favor through sacrifices, which are based on superstition and only cause unnecessary anxiety. To the Epicureans, the life and behavior of the gods served as a model for human beings to follow.

The aim of human life is to attain the undisturbed peace of mind and tranquility of the gods. This constitutes true happiness, and it is realized through pleasure. Contrary to popular belief, the Epicureans did not encourage physical pleasures, but pleasures of the mind or soul. They understood pleasure as the absence of bodily pain and of disquiet of the soul. It is peace of mind, a tranquil, undisturbable existence. This is achieved by living a life of prudence, virtue, and justice and being in complete control of all the physical pleasures, the passions, desires, and needs that might be a hindrance to the tranquility of the soul. The Epicurean life was one of moderate asceticism, with desires maintained to the simplest minimum, self-control, and independence from all externals, a withdrawal from the world. Epicureans were quietists; they obeyed the civic laws and customs and did not create any problems or disturbances to society, but they also did not accept any. Unlike the Stoics, who encouraged public involvement and service, the Epicureans advocated the avoidance of public office and political life and were not concerned for the welfare of the general populace. This does not imply that they espoused a life of hermetic solitude, but a life shared with friends. The Epicureans considered friendship an important aspect of the happy, tranquil, undisturbable life, but friendship shared with a close small circle of like-minded people.

Epicureanism spread throughout the Hellenistic-Roman world and was popular in Rome during the 1st century B.C.E., but it never achieved the wide popularity and influence of Stoicism. Unlike Stoicism, which changed and developed throughout the Hellenistic-Roman period, Epicureanism remained unchanged. It continued to adhere to the teachings of its founder who was venerated, and to meet in small exclusive circles of philosopher friends. The school was neither influenced by other philosophies nor did it influence others in any significant way. In the late 1st–early 2nd century C.E., the Epicureans' teaching of the quiet unpolitical life and the denial that the gods had any involvement in the world caused them to be looked upon with disfavor and to be criticized as irreligious.

Middle Platonism

The Platonic revival, which had begun on a modest scale in the latter part of the 1st century B.C.E., developed by the 2nd century C.E. into a philosophical movement known as Middle Platonism. This was a time when the Hellenistic-Roman world was witnessing a succession of barbarian invasions, bloody civil wars, various recurring plagues, famines, and economic crises. Middle Platonism attempted to provide a solution to the problem of human destiny and salvation through a philosophical understanding of the universe. The movement produced a group of Middle Platonic philosophers that combined in their thought elements of Aristotelian logic, Stoic psychology and ethics, and Pythagorean mysticism, in varying degrees. Despite its loosely knit and highly diversified character, there exists some measure of uniformity in Middle Platonic speculation that makes possible a few general remarks. The most significant contribution of the movement was to bring together and equate the supreme Divine Mind of Aristotle and the Platonic world of Forms and Ideas.

Middle Platonism postulates a hierarchy of three divine primary beings, at the head of which is the Divine Mind or God — the first principle of reality. The supreme God is often called the One or the Good, and is a simple, changeless, and transcendent being, having no direct contact with the material world and inaccessible to the human mind in this life, except in rare and brief flashes of illumination. In the supreme Mind, the Middle Platonists placed the Platonic ideas, the eternal forms which, according to Plato, constitute the archetypal models of all existing things in the universe. These forms or patterns exist in the mind of the first God and are the models upon which the cosmos is created. Being unchanging and transcendent, the Supreme God does not create. He derives from himself a second Mind or God, subordinate to and dependent on the first God, who creates and governs the world. The third principle in the Middle Platonic hierarchy is the World Soul. Human souls, according to the Middle Platonists, are parts of the Divine that have descended into the material world and have become embodied. Thus, the aim in life is to free oneself from the world of matter and to return to the Divine. The Middle Platonic concept of the soul, nature, and destiny influenced later philosophic thought, both pagan and Christian. Of particular importance were the views of Numenius and Albinus.

Numenius of Apamea (ca. 150-200 C.E.) was a Pythagoreanizing

All we got a view

Platonist. He adopted a synthesis of Platonic and Pythagorean doctrine. In agreement with Middle Platonic thought, Numenius posits a divine triad, a supreme Mind or God whom he calls Father or the Good, a second Mind or demiurge, and the created third God or the World Soul. The first God, or the Good, is simple, eternal, changeless, transcendent, and at leisure; i.e., he concerns himself only with the intelligible universe and takes no active part in the formation or affairs of the sensible world. From his essence, without diminishing it in any way, is derived the demiurge, who participates in the activities of both the spiritual and phenomenal worlds. He contemplates the Good, but is also interested in bringing order and structure into matter. Because of his double interest, he is double or twofold, for although the demiurge effects order out of the chaotic nature of matter, he is distracted by matter and his interest is divided. Thus a part of the demiurge is always in contemplation of the Good, and the other part is concerned with the creation and governance of the world. The creating part of the demiurge becomes the soul of the material world. Numenius taught that there are two world souls. The contemplating part of the demiurge is the good world soul; and the creating part, because it concerns itself with matter, which Numenius considers evil, is the evil world soul. This soul is in constant opposition with Providence or the good world soul, which strives to perfect matter. Therefore, Numenius, agreeing with the Pythagorean view, claims that the sensible world was created by a mingling of matter and divinity, of Providence and chance, from the yielding of matter to the persuasion of God.

The human soul, according to Numenius, is a divine being, a fragment or particle of the demiurge, indistinguishably identical with its source. It contains within itself the whole intelligible world, the gods, the demons, the Good, and all prior kinds of Being. Like their source, all souls are immortal. Individual souls are drawn to the material world and into bodies by the same desire to bring matter into structure and order, which characterizes the activity of the second divinity. However, since Numenius considered matter evil, any involvement of the soul with matter is considered by him an evil act. Similar to the demiurge, the individual soul is double by virtue of its essence and activity. Numenius defines it as a number, a divine form or idea in movement, halfway between nature and what is beyond nature, indivisible in that it is a monad, divisible in that it is a dyad. Thus, the individual possesses two souls, a rational and an irrational. The rational soul, which is the individual's *nous* or mind, is derived from the second

42

divinity. The irrational part, which contains the various faculties of the individual, is caused by matter, and considered by Numenius as the author and mistress of the irrational soul. It is acquired by the higher soul or *nous* during the descent to earth and appears, in Numenius's view, as the acquisition of a vaporous envelope from the planets that accumulates around *nous*.

Numenius's doctrine of the descent and ascent of the soul is an allegorical interpretation of myths found in the works of Plato, and in particular the myths of Er in the 10th book of the *Republic*. According to Numenius, the soul descends from heaven, which is for him the sphere of the fixed stars, through its northern gate, the Tropic of Cancer. From there it travels through the seven planetary spheres. Between the gate of heaven and the first planetary sphere, each soul, in varying degrees, loses the memory of its existence in the intelligible world. As it passes through each sphere, it acquires an ethereal envelopment or layer and the disposition peculiar to each planet. In Saturn's sphere, the soul receives reason and understanding; in Jupiter's, the ability to act; in Mars's, its boldness; in the sun's sphere, sense-perception and imagination; in Venus's, the impulse of passion; in Mercury's, the ability to speak and to interpret; and in the sphere of the moon, the function of molding and increasing bodies. After the lunar sphere, the soul enters the earth, where it receives the last touches or layers of its earthly garment — the body. At the death of the body, the soul again traverses the path through the planetary spheres and gives back to each that which it received on its downward journey. In each sphere, the soul's life on earth is reviewed and its fate decided. If it is found worthy, it is permitted to ascend to heaven through the southern gate, the Tropic of Capricorn, and to live among the gods in eternal bliss. On the other hand, if the soul is found wanting, it is sent to a region of chastisement, the atmosphere between the moon and the earth, which Numenius calls the region above the waters. There it hovers, tormented by and struggling with the physical demons, until it is once again attracted to a new body. This new body is dependent on the faculty that the soul developed the most in its previous life. If it followed the dictates of the body rather than those of reason, it could become assimilated to an irrational creature. Eventually, however, the soul is released from the cycle of birth. After a series of repeated generations or incarnations, it is finally purified and returns to its place in the divine.

Incarnation was regarded by Numenius as a fall of the soul and thus evil. Nonetheless, he considered it necessary for the maintenance and organization of the body, without which it would disperse and scatter into atoms. Life in the body is a long, hard battle with the two souls of the individual in constant conflict to gain dominance. Peace and happiness are attained when the soul abandons the world of sense and achieves a relationship with the Good, alone with the alone. The approach to the Good is very difficult. While the soul is in the body, this can best be accomplished by detaching itself completely from everything sensible and contemplating the divine. After intense waiting and concentration, the soul arrives at the understanding of what is true reality.

Significant and one of the most interesting of the Middle Platonists was Albinus, a contemporary of Numenius. Albinus represents an Aristotelianizing form of Platonism, He interpreted Plato by means of Aristotle's logic and terminology, to which he added several Stoic doctrines. Similar to Numenius, Albinus postulates three divine principles: the first God or Mind, also called the Good; the second God or Universal Intellect; and the World Soul. As in Numenius's thinking, he does not make a clear distinction between the second God and the World Soul. The first God in Albinus's triad is identified both with the Good of Plato's *Republic* and the First Mover of Aristotle's *Metaphysics;* he is "forever thinking upon himself" and is "identical with his own ideas," the intelligible ideas which are exemplary causes or paradigms of all existing things. Albinus emphasized the superiority of the first God who is the final and efficient cause of all things, actualizing and bringing into effective existence the other two divine principles — the Cosmic Mind and the World Soul. These two principles are formed and made active and useful by the first God by turning in contemplation towards him and his intelligizing acts or thoughts. Although the Good causes movement, he is unmoved, remaining beyond space, the supra-cosmic mind or *nous*, eternal, incorporeal, perfect in himself, ineffable, and beyond all human thought comprehended by the mind alone. Albinus describes the Good's transcendence through the use of an undeveloped "negative theology," stating what he is not rather than what he is — similar to that used to describe the First Hypothesis in Plato's *Parmenides*. Despite his remote transcendence, the first God or Good is still a *nous or* mind, the head of the hierarchy of being, not beyond it.

Albinus claims that the world is eternal. It has no temporal beginning but is perpetually being formed and governed by the second God, the active universal mind who, like the first God, is identical with his ideas or patterns. Similar to Numenius, Albinus divides the world into spheres: the celestial or sphere of the fixed stars, the seven planetary spheres, and the earth, each of which is inhabited by intelligible living beings, souls. The most perfect souls are those of the fixed stars and of the planets and are considered as gods. In Stoic fashion, Albinus states that they were created by God from a fiery substance. Below the planetary spheres, in the atmosphere and on the earth in each of the four elements so that no part of the world is without a soul, are subordinate gods or demons, both visible and invisible, known as "begotten gods." To these gods was committed the ordering and guidance of the sublunary world and the creation of all mortal beings, the creatures of the air, of the water, and of the earth, and the giving of oracles and dreams. The human race also belongs to the earthly creatures, but it is so closely related to the divine that the first God took a special interest in its creation. The molding or fashioning of the human body was assigned to the subordinate gods, but the human soul was formed by God. Like the Soul of the World, the individual souls were not created. They were formed or brought into order and made active by God by turning them in contemplation towards himself and his intelligizing acts. After putting the individual souls in order, he sent them down to their earthly habitations.

Albinus's doctrine of the soul is vague and incoherent. He gives two main reasons for the soul's embodiment, without any attempt to reconcile the two, or any apparent awareness of the difficulties existing between them. Incarnation, he claims, is due either to a law of nature established by the divine, or to a voluntary action on the part of the soul — its licentiousness or love for the body. There is a very strong affinity between body and soul, like fire and asphalt.[74] Albinus speaks of the soul as having two parts, a rational and an irrational. The former is concerned with the suprasensible, the latter with the sensible. As in Numenius, the two parts of the soul are always at war with each other, but Albinus does not take as pessimistic a view of the material world. He does not posit the existence of an evil World Soul, nor does he explicitly identify matter as evil. The rational part of the soul is divine, eternal, immortal, indestructible, and incorporeal. It is divine because it was formed or put in order by the first God and because it existed before it entered the body, and it will remain after the

---

74. For a detailed discussion of Albinus's reasons for the soul's embodiment, see Tripolitis, 33-34 and n. 231.

body's death. Thus, it can be assumed that it is eternal, immortal, and indestructible. Concerning the irrational part of the soul, Albinus firmly asserts that it, as well as the soul of all irrational animals, is mortal. Its mortality is attributed to the fact that it was not formed by the first God, but by the subordinate gods. Each part of the soul, the rational and irrational, is distinct and self-subsistent and lodged in a different part of the body. The rational part is confined to the head, and the two faculties that comprise the irrational part, that of desire and anger, are localized in the liver and heart, respectively.

Adhering closely to the thought of Plato, Albinus states that the aim of every individual is to become as much like God as is humanly possible. Assimilation to God is achieved through knowledge of him, which, according to Albinus, is achieved in three ways: through the way of abstraction or negation, the way of analogy, and the way of eminence or gradual ascent, which is accomplished through contemplation. The contemplative state is reached through the perfection or purification of the soul, i.e., the practice of the cardinal virtues. Albinus identifies the virtues and assigns a different one to each part of the soul. Prudence is the perfection of the rational part of the soul, temperance or self-control that of the desiring faculty, and courage the purification of the faculty of anger. The fourth virtue, justice, is the general virtue. It is the power that brings together and harmonizes the different faculties of the soul and brings them under the influence of reason. Thus all three virtues must be practiced simultaneously, for only in this way can the soul be completely purified and achieve likeness to God.

Numenius and Albinus anticipated several of the views and positions of the Neo-Platonists beginning with Plotinus and the early Christian theologians. In their views of the divine hierarchy and the individual soul are found the rudiments of concepts that were more fully developed and systematized in different ways by both pagan and Christian thinkers.

Chapter II

MITHRAISM

A. The Myth and Origins of Mithras

Mithra was an Indo-Iranian deity whose earliest recorded evidence is found in a 14th-century B.C.E. treaty between the Hittites and their neighbors, the Mitanni of Upper Mesopotamia. In the document, Mithra is invoked as a guarantor of the treaty and his name is recorded as "Mitra," meaning literally "treaty" or "covenant." Mithra's name is also found in the early sacred writings of India, where he is frequently referred to as Mitra, and in the holy books of the Persians, where he is called Mithra. Both in the Indian and Persian literature, he is an agent of the supreme being, the Indian Varuna and the Persian Ahura Mazda, who ordained the cosmos and maintains its order. Mithra is the mediator between mankind and the supreme deity, heaven and earth. He is a divinity of light, but subordinate to the supreme deity. As a divinity of the upper regions, he is all-seeing, and thus an enforcer of oaths and treaties. Mithra was greatly revered by the Persians and rose to great prominence. With the expansion of the Persian Empire in the 5th century, the worship of Mithra spread throughout Asia Minor. In Asia Minor, principally in Cilicia, sometime in the last two centuries B.C.E., Mithra was hellenized, was given the name Mithras, a Greek form of Mithra, and became the central deity of a cult. It is thought that Mithras's cult was introduced into the Hellenistic-Roman world by Cilician pirates who had allied with Mithridates, king of Pontus, against the Romans in the so-called Mithridatic Wars. Mithridates was defeated by Pompey ca. 66 B.C.E. Some of the Cilician pirates were captured and taken to Rome, where they introduced the Mithraic mysteries. The cult began to spread rapidly throughout the empire in the late 1st century C.E. It reached its climax in the 3rd century, at which time its *mithraea,* the Mithraic sanctuaries, were found from one end of the empire to the other. In the Hellenistic-Roman world, Mithraism was more than a cult; it was a mystery religion in the full sense.

The literary evidence of the cult in the West is scanty. As in the cults of the time, the teachings of Mithras were known only to the initiates and were never made public. Although the 3rd-century Neoplatonist Porphyry and other authorities claim that a number of writings on Mithraism existed, none of this material is extant.[1] Knowledge of Mithraism is derived almost exclusively from nonliterary sources, primarily from the iconography found in the mithraea. The mithraea were small dark narrow caves, built either underground or constructed to resemble underground caves, with room for about 20 devotees who sat on benches placed against the side walls. The caves represent the cosmos and their vaulted ceilings the celestial vault, the heavens with the zodiac. Frequently, the ceilings were decorated with stars, and special effects were used to suggest the presence of the deity. Most sanctuaries contained a niche in the back wall, and all were decorated with iconographic scenes of Mithraic activity. These scenes vary from sanctuary to sanctuary, but one scene common to all the mithraea is the *tauroctony,* or the bull-slaying scene. It is found on the back wall, in the niche if there is one, of every sanctuary and portrayed what was regarded as Mithras's greatest accomplishment.

The bull-slaying scene, either a relief carved from stone or a fresco, depicts the god as young, supple, and strong, dressed in Persian clothes and wearing a Phrygian cap. He is turned to the right and, with his left knee on the bull's back, is pinning down the animal. The bull is crouching, and its right foreleg is sharply bent. Mithras holds the bull's head backward by its mouth or nostril with his left hand, and with the sword or dagger in his right hand thrusts it into the bull's flank. From the collapsing bull's tail spring ears of corn. Above the relief or painting was often an arched border with the signs of the zodiac. The rising sun and setting moon are represented on the top left and right hand corner of the scene, respectively. Several other figures are also depicted. A raven, considered a messenger from the region of the sun, is found over Mithras's right shoulder; a dog

---

1. Esmé Wynne-Tyson, *Mithras: The Fellow in the Cap,* 2nd ed. (New York: Barnes & Noble, 1972), 30.

and a snake are seen licking the blood from the bull's wound; and a scorpion attacks the bull from beneath. Sometimes beneath the bull are also found a bowl and a squatting lion.

Two figures that are rarely absent from the bull-slaying scene are the twin gods Cautes and Cautopates, shown situated on either side of the bull. They are both dressed in clothes similar to those of Mithras, and each carries a flaming torch. Cautes, the symbol of the rising sun, carries his torch pointing upward, and Cautopates, symbolizing the setting sun, has his torch pointing downward. Cautes, with the uplifted torch, is usually depicted under the moon, and Cautopates under the sun. The two gods are understood as epithets of Mithras. A 4th-century c.e. text of Pseudo-Dionysius the Areopagite states that the two torch-bearers form a trinity with Mithras. Cautes represents the morning sun, Mithras the sun at noon, and Cautopates the setting sun.[2] Thus, Mithras is the rising, noon, and setting sun, and his influence and power are revealed daily.[3]

There is scant information from the ancient literary sources about the meaning of the bull-slaying scene, thus making its interpretation difficult. Hellenistic cosmology appears to be present in the scene, but there is also vegetative or creative symbolism in the ears of corn that sprang from the bull's tail. Unfortunately, without any extant literature, the meaning of the various symbols can only be inferred from the pictorial representation. Modern scholars have proffered a number of explanations. Some present a philosophical perspective,[4] while others emphasize a Hellenistic-Roman astrological/astronomical explanation,[5] but none are decisive. All that can be said with some certainty is that the slaying of the bull has a soteriological significance. It was an act of salvation that is an important aspect in all the ancient mystery religions and cults. This is

2. M. J. Vermaseren, *Mithras, the Secret God* (New York: Barnes & Noble, 1963), 72-73. The basic work on Mithraism is Franz Cumont, *The Mysteries of Mithra* (New York: Dover, 1956). Cumont's iconographical interpretations have been challenged in recent scholarship. Vermaseren's work updates Cumont's in light of new discoveries; his interpretations are more cautious than Cumont's.

3. Vermaseren, *Mithras*, 73.

4. See esp. Reinhold Merkelbach, *Mithras* (Königstein: Hain, 1984); and Robert Turcan, *Mithras Platonicus: Recherches sur l'hellénisation philosophique de Mithra.* EPRO 47 (Leiden: E. J. Brill, 1975).

5. See esp. Michael P. Speidel, *Mithras-Orion: Greek Hero and Roman Army God.* EPRO 81 (Leiden: E. J. Brill, 1980); and David Ulansey, *The Origins of the Mithraic Mysteries* (New York: Oxford University Press, 1989).

implied in an inscription found in the mithraeum of Santa Prisca, Rome, and dated to 202 C.E.: "Us too you have saved by shedding blood which grants eternity."[6]

Two other scenes frequently found in the mithraea and considered of major importance to the religion are the sacred meal and the rock birth of Mithras. The sacred meal is second in importance only to the bull-slaying act, to which it is a complement. It is often found on the back of a reversible relief, with the bull-slaying scene on the front.[7] The meal took place in a cave on the bull's skin. In most scenes, Mithras reclines or sits with the sun, depicted as a deity, eating the flesh of the bull and drinking its blood. Representations and verses found in mithraea of the late 2nd–early 3rd century C.E. reveal that bread and wine sometimes replaced the meat and blood.[8] On some monuments, Mithras and the Sun are the only participants, while on others their followers and representatives are also shown. The sacred meal took place at the end of Mithras's stay on earth, after completing a number of arduous heroic and miraculous deeds for the good of humankind, from which he always emerged victorious.[9] Following the meal, Mithras and the sun-god ascend to the heavens in the Sun's chariot. Unlike the gods of the cults popular during the Hellenistic-Roman period who annually were born and died, Mithras was born once, accomplished his work laboring for goodness, truth, and justice, and returned to the heavens from where he guides and protects his followers. His heroic achievements are often equated to the labors of Hercules.[10] The sacred meal was re-enacted at the celebration of the cult's mysteries, and was considered the central act. Its effect and how it was carried out in the rites is uncertain.[11]

The other important Mithraic event was Mithras's birth, which was considered a miraculous, cosmic occurrence. He was born from a genera-

---

6. Vermaseren, *Mithras*, 177. See also Walter Burkert, *Ancient Mystery Cults* (Cambridge, Mass.: Harvard University Press, 1987), 111ff. An excellent critical analysis of the archaeological finds and their various interpretations is Roger Beck, "Mithraism since Franz Cumont," *ANRW* 17/4 (New York: Walter de Gruyter, 1984), 2002-2115. For his understanding of the inscriptions' importance, see 2029.

7. Vermaseren, *Mithras*, 99; Beck, 2083.

8. Vermaseren, *Mithras*, 101-3.

9. Mithras's various deeds on earth are discussed in Vermaseren, *Mithras*, 79-105.

10. A. D. Nock, "The Genius of Mithraism," *JRS* 27 (1937): 112 and n. 24.

11. Beck, 2083.

tive rock, forced out as if by some hidden magic power.[12] His birthday is celebrated on December 25, the day of the winter solstice. Mithras is most frequently depicted as a young boy emerging from the rock wearing only a Phrygian cap and holding a dagger and a torch in his raised hands. The rock symbolized the firmament from which light descends to earth, and Mithras the new begetter of light.[13] Sometimes Mithras's birth is represented near a spring that became the eternal spring, a source of life-giving water.[14] On some representations, Mithras's birth is attended by shepherds, and on others by the brothers Cautes and Cautopates. A number of scenes depict Mithras emerging from the rock holding the cosmic globe in his one hand and with the other touching the circle of the zodiac that forms a ring around him. This depiction reveals Mithras as a cosmic ruler, a *kosmokrator*, with the power to control the cosmic sphere. As in the bull-slaying scene, Mithras's birth has as its fundamental basis elements of Hellenistic-Roman astrology and astronomy.

B. Mysteries of Mithras

Access to the Mithraic community and its mysteries was exclusively for men; women were always excluded. Iconographic and inscriptional evidence reveal that membership in the cult came primarily from the ranks of the Roman army, but also included members of the imperial government as well as merchants and slaves. The cult consisted of seven grades of initiation through which the initiate slowly advanced. Most initiates did not advance beyond the first level, because of lack of either dedication, necessary education, or the funds required to progress to the higher grades.[15] Prior to initiation, an individual went through a period of preparatory instruction, of which the form or its nature is unknown. Before the rite of initiation, the initiate had to take a solemn oath that he would not reveal anything about the rite. The initiation was conducted under the direction of the *Pater*, the Father of the Community, an individual who had attained

12. Vermaseren, *Mithras*, 75.
13. Vermaseren, *Mithras*, 75.
14. Vermaseren, *Mithras*, 88.
15. Vermaseren, *Mithras*, 138. The data on the initiation and the various grades of the cult are derived mainly from Vermaseren's work, 129-53, which is considered one of the best surveys on the subject.

the highest grade in the Mithraic cult, and *Heliodromus,* the Courier of the Sun, who was one grade below the Father.

Initiation into the mysteries was conducted within a mithraeum. Evidence from the mithraea, some not well preserved, and scornful controversial statements found in Christian literary sources reveal that the initiates had to undergo severe trials and extreme tests of endurance.[16] A number of scenes convey the fears that the initiates experienced. Included are scenes that show the initiates blindfolded, some with their hands tied together, and led through a series of ordeals. In other scenes, an initiate is seen lying on the ground as if dead and waiting for a symbolic new life. There are indications of purification through washings, ordeals of heat and cold, and scourging. Initiates also had to fast and undergo periods of abstinence. Because of the paucity of evidence about the details in either iconography or literature, the little that is known cannot accurately be correlated to the various grades of initiation. After completing the ordeals, the initiate is branded either on both hands or on the forehead. The branding is his identification as a member of the cult. Following this act, the initiate clasps his right hand with that of the Father's as a pledge of fidelity and alliance, both in this life and in the hereafter. With the joining of right hands, he is welcomed and confirmed as a member into the Mithraic community, and is now considered a son of the Father and a brother of the other fellow initiates. More than in any other cult, the Mithraic initiate was a member of a closely knit family that aided each other; each member was protected by his victorious god both in this life and the next.

As the initiate gained knowledge and insight into the principles of the cult and fulfilled the various requirements, he advanced through each grade and successively received the titles Corax, the Raven; Nymphus, the Bride; Miles, the Soldier; Leo, the Lion; Perses, the Persian; Heliodromus, the Courier of the Sun; and Pater, the Father. The first three grades are considered preparatory, and their members, Corax, Nymphus, and Miles were called "attendants" and served as such at the sacred meal. Those of Leo, Perses, and Heliodromus were full members and were called "participants" and took full part in the sacred meal. In some representations, however, Corax, an attendant, is represented as a participant, and Leo, a participant, is depicted as an attendant. Thus it appears that the attendants could also be participants and the participants could be attendants. Each of the

16. Vermaseren, *Mithras,* 131-36.

seven grades of initiation had its own ritual with preparations, requirements, and ordeals. Of the little that is known about these activities, much
of it is deduced from the iconography. Through the symbolic iconographical representation of each grade a number of attempts have been made to
associate each grade with a physical element and with a planet. None, however, has received total acceptance.[17]

Corax, the lowest or first grade, is often symbolized with a caduceus,
understood as a sign for the planet Mercury, the grade's protector. Its element is generally understood to be air. Nymphus's emblem consists of a
lamp and a diadem, a symbol for the planet Venus, the protector of the
grade. Venus was understood to have two aspects, morning star and evening star. The lamp represents both Venus as the bringer of light and the
grade under its protection as the "new light" that proceeds from a new and
closer relationship with Mithras. Nymphus is generally understood to represent the element of water. The symbols of Miles include a military
kitbag, a lance, and a helmet, and were under the protection of Mars, the
god of war. Evidence shows that initiation into the grade of Miles included
the offering of a wreath on the point of a sword to the initiate, who hum-
bly rejects it, saying that "Mithras alone is my wreath; my wreath rests in
my god."[18] With this declaration, the initiate assumes the responsibility,
like Mithras before him, to fight against evil. Since Corax and Nymphus
represent air and water, respectively, it is assumed that Miles symbolized
the earth, but no definite proof of this exists.[19]

The Leo grade represented a very significant stage in the initiate's
progress through the mysteries, as evidenced by the numerous epigraphic
references to this grade, more than all others put together.[20] It was the
transitional point between the first three grades, the preparatory state and
membership. Leo's symbols were a fire shovel, the Egyptian sacred rattle, a
sign associated with lions in Egyptian lore, and the thunderbolt of Jupiter,
the grade's protector.[21] Leo was considered to have a fiery nature because

17. Beck, 2092 and n, 142.
18. Vermaseren, *Mithras,* 145.
19. Vermaseren, *Mithras,* 144.
20. R. L. Gordon, "Reality, evocation and boundary in the Mysteries of Mithras," *JMS* 3
(1980): 3. For the importance of *Leo,* see 32-41. Gordon's article (19-99) attempts to explain
the use of the various representations of the grades by tracing their significance in the Hellenistic-Roman tradition and beliefs.
21. Gordon, 35.

the sun entered the constellation Leo during the hottest time of year, the height of summer.[22] The grade represented the element of fire. Initiates into this grade underwent a baptism or purification of fire. Also included in the initiation was the cleansing of the initiate's hands and tongue with honey instead of water. The purifying fire transformed the initiate into a new person, one morally purified and sanctified. A responsibility of the members of the grade of Leo was to burn the incense that had been offered by other members, whose identity, due to lack of evidence, is unknown.[23]

The fifth grade, Perses, was under the protection of the moon, which it personified. Its objects were the sickle and the scythe. Like the grade of Leo, the initiate's hands were cleansed with honey, but in the Perses grade it was administered in his capacity as the guardian of the fruits and plants. In antiquity, honey was considered a preservative, and in Perses it symbolized the preservation of vegetation.[24] Heliodromus was the earthly representative of the sun-god and was placed under his protection. Its emblem consisted of a whip, a radiate halo, and a torch and represented the sun's daily journey across the skies in his chariot, urging the horses on with his whip. The last and highest grade of the cult, Pater, is the representative of the god Mithras on earth. He is the teacher of the initiates and the high priest chosen by his fellow initiates, and serves as their Father and protector of the community interests. His responsibilities include accepting new members into the cult, and presiding over the initiations into each grade and at the consecration of every new mithraeum. Pater's symbols are Mithras's Phrygian cap, the staff and ring, and the sickle of Saturn. The staff and ring symbolize his wisdom as teacher, and the sickle indicates that he is under the guardianship of Saturn. At the re-enactment of the sacred meal, the farewell banquet of Mithras and the Sun, the Pater and Heliodromus, respectively, represented Mithras and the sun-god.

The seven grades of Mithraic initiation took place in the mithraeum, the cave which symbolized the cosmos, but due to the lack of clear evidence, the exact significance of the initiation is not known. Most interpreters understand the grades as a spiritual, purifying journey, the gradual spiritual progress of the soul while still in the body, achieved by fulfilling the ritual and moral requirements of each grade. The Mithraists believed

---

22. Gordon, 33-34.
23. Gordon, 36-37; also for the importance of incense-burning in the cult.
24. Vermaseren, *Mithras,* 150.

that the soul descended into the cosmos from the sun through the seven planetary spheres. As it passed through the spheres, it received an attribute from each, which it discarded on its ascent back to the heavens after the death of the body. The seven grades symbolize the soul's return through the spheres and are imaged, according to the 2nd-century Christian polemicist Celsus, as a ladder with seven rungs.[25] As it passed through each, the soul discarded that which it had received in its descent. The ascending order of the planets found in Celsus and in some representations — Saturn, Venus, Jupiter, Mercury, Mars, Moon, and Sun — does not conform with the sequence of the planets when they serve as protectors of the seven grades of the cult — Mercury, Venus, Mars, Jupiter, Moon, Sun, and Saturn. The former sequence is based on that of the days of the week and in inverse order to the accepted system of Hellenistic-Roman astrology. In the Mithraic planetary order associated with the seven grades, the sequence contradicts the accepted Hellenistic-Roman order based on the view of each planet's distance from the earth — Saturn, Jupiter, Mars, Sun, Venus, Mercury, and Moon — and is considered to be based on the old Iranian sequence.[26]

In addition to the rites of initiation, the Mithraic rituals included daily religious services, the burning of perpetual fire at the altars, and prayers addressed to the Sun three times a day — at dawn, noon, and dusk. The daily services frequently included special sacrifices of which almost nothing is known. Sunday, the day of the Sun, was especially sacred, as was the 25th of December, the birthday of the god Mithras. This day was celebrated by sacred festivals. There were also communal meals commemorating the farewell banquet of Mithras and the Sun, and votives were continuously offered either in appreciation for the god's aid in a time of crisis or to ask for his protection. To his followers, Mithras was an energetic, helpful, and efficacious god.

25. Celsus's view is quoted by Origen in his response to Celsus. See Origen, *Contra Celsum,* trans. Henry Chadwick (1965, repr. Cambridge: Cambridge University Press, 1980), 334 and n. 2.

26. Burkert, *Ancient Mystery Cults,* 160, n. 106.

C. Influence and Development
in the Hellenistic-Roman Age

The worship of Mithras was introduced to the West ca. 70 B.C.E. By the end of the 1st century C.E., it had begun to spread throughout the empire, and by the middle of the 3rd century it had become the most important of the contemporary cults. It was especially widespread and popular in Rome (where there were more than 600 mithraea), Ostia, and the northern frontier provinces and the seaports, but for some unknown reason the cult by-passed Greece proper. At the beginning of the 4th century C.E., Mithras, the foreign god of the departed or emigrated Cilicians, had, as the *Sol invictus,* the invincible Sun, become the official god of the Roman state. Mithraism's very early adherents were slaves and tradesmen. By the 2nd century, it had become popular among the members of the Roman army, and by the 3rd century, its adherents included members of the Roman aristocracy and its imperial court. Mithraism's emphasis on justice, truthfulness, loyalty, and courage made it especially appealing to the Roman legions, which served as the principal agent of its dissemination and constituted the major portion of its membership. Mithraea were found wherever the Roman armies were stationed, along the entire length of the Roman frontier as far as Britain and the mountains of Scotland. One of the reasons proffered regarding Mithraism's absence from the Greek mainland was that few Roman soldiers were either recruited or stationed there.[27]

Mithraism's influence and development were much enhanced by the patronage of the imperial officials and emperors, and by Mithras's ability to adapt himself to the various regional gods and his willingness to accept other gods. As the religion spread throughout the Roman provinces, Mithras assumed the characteristics of the god of each province. In Gaul, he was equated with the god Apollo, and in Germany and France with Mercury. Some representations in German and Roman mithraea reveal Mithras as Atlas supporting the vault of heaven.[28] Moreover, Mithraism accepted individuals who worshipped other gods in addition to Mithras. Statues dedicated to other gods have been found in a number of mithraea. The empire's interest in and movement to sun worship in the

27. Speidel, 46.
28. Vermaseren, *Mithras,* 112-16.

late 3rd–early 4th centuries also served to reinforce Mithraism's influence and dissemination, since Mithras had always been associated with the sun-god.

The cult's first major period of influence came during the reign of the emperor Aurelian (270-275). Aurelian believed that the sun had granted him victory over Zenobia, queen of Palmyra, in 273, and shortly thereafter, in the same year, he erected a large temple to the god whom he worshipped as the only heavenly, almighty, and divine power.[29] The sun was proclaimed the universal god of the empire, and Aurelian promoted the cult of *Sol invictus,* raised it to the status of an official cult, and attempted to establish a quasi sun-god monotheism. Aurelian's sun-god religion was not the religion of Mithras, but the Mithraic cult took advantage of Mithras's association with the sun.

Mithraism's second and greatest period of influence was during the early 4th century. In 308, Diocletian (284-305), who had recently abdicated, held a conference with his successors at Carnuntum on the borders of the empire. At the end of the conference, they consecrated a large altar with an inscription proclaiming Mithras the invincible sun-god and the protector of their rule, and restored the Carnuntum mithraeum. The dedication established Mithras as the official god of the Roman state, replacing the general sun-god of Aurelian. During this period, Mithraism was at its peak and it appeared as if it might become the sole state religion, but Constantine's triumph in 312 as sole ruler of the empire shattered its hopes. It was Christianity that finally became the religion of the empire. Mithraism's hopes of becoming the state religion were rekindled, briefly, during the reign of the emperor Julian (361-363), who from childhood had been a devotee of the sun-god. In his adult years he was initiated into the Mithraic cult and attained its highest grade, that of Pater. During his reign, Julian did all that was possible to encourage the triumph of the cult, but his reign was short-lived. By the end of the 4th century, Mithraism had lost all its power and influence.

29. Vermaseren, *Mithras,* 187.

D. Mithraism's Decline and Disappearance

For more than 200 years, Mithraism was a formidable competitor of Christianity.[30] Unlike Christianity, it enjoyed the favor of the imperial administration, almost from the time of its arrival in the West, as well as the state's support for the building and maintenance of its monuments. From the late 1st century C.E., Mithraic sanctuaries and monuments flourished throughout the vast area of Roman occupation. Yet despite its popularity and influence on the Romans, by the end of the 4th century, Mithraism had almost completely disappeared from Roman soil. The reasons for its disappearance were both external and internal. Externally, the first blow to Mithraism came in 324 with Constantine's acceptance of Christianity as an official religion of the empire. Although it was not persecuted, Mithraism was not recognized as previously, but merely tolerated. Constantine's successors, however, were hostile to the cult and actively persecuted it. During this time, the cult had many sympathizers, but only a few true followers.[31] Mithraism enjoyed a brief revival during the short-lived reign of Julian, who was a devotee and initiate of Mithras. Following Julian, there was a period of toleration until 382, when the emperor Gratian (367-383) had Mithras's sanctuaries sacked of their wealth, ordered them closed, and withdrew all state support for the cult's maintenance. Finally, the emperor Theodosius in an edict in 391 forbade all pagan worship, had all the temples closed, and proclaimed that anyone practicing a pagan religion would be severely punished. Mithraism survived in a few remote regions, but by the early 5th century it had been abandoned in the Latin world.

Internally, Mithraism had several weaknesses that, even had Christianity not prevailed, would have caused it eventually to disappear or become the special devotion of but a very few.[32] One was its narrow exclusiveness, its refusal to include women in any participation in the cult, which thus deprived itself of the group that is most loyal and devoted to religion.[33] By excluding one half of the population, the cult eliminated the possibility of

30. The extent of Mithraism's rivalry with Christianity has been questioned recently; see Beck, 2095-96.

31. Vermaseren, *Mithras*, 189.

32. Nock, *JRS* 27 (1937): 113.

33. Leonard Patterson, *Mithraism and Christianity: A Study in Comparative Religion* (Cambridge: Cambridge University Press, 1921), 90-91.

attaining the status of a world religion.[34] Mithraism's remarkable ability to adapt to any environment in which it found itself, in the long run, proved to be damaging. The cult was the most syncretistic of all the cults and religions, combining within itself the most diverse and incongruous elements. This caused it to lose its strength, definiteness, and cohesion.[35] Finally, Mithraism did not have an established clerical hierarchy or a professional clergy, nor a developed organizational structure. Each town had its mithraeum with its Pater, but there is no evidence of a central organization or an established set of common rules, important factors in the survival of Judaism and Christianity even as minorities in a hostile environment. Moreover, Mithraism was closely linked to the social structure of the state, and when it lost its support, Mithraism ceased to exist.

Example

Frontier Days:
Baptists & Methodists
tried to established
religion.

Methodist - sent out circuit riders
to established churches

Baptists - most democratic
religious institution.
↳ selects own leaders based on
a common understanding

---

34. John G. Gager, *Kingdom and Community: The Social World of Early Christianity* (Englewood Cliffs: Prentice-Hall, 1975), 133-34.

35. Patterson, 91.

Chapter III

HELLENISTIC JUDAISM

The cosmopolitan and transnational culture of the Hellenistic-Roman world that fostered changes in Greek attitudes towards the traditional gods, their influence and importance, and the development of new forms of religious experiences that now fulfilled the needs of the individual was also significant in the development of the life and thought of the Jewish people, and especially of Diaspora Judaism. This chapter concentrates on the hellenization of Diaspora Judaism, designated as Hellenistic Judaism, and on its contribution to the larger Jewish community and to the development of early Christianity.

A. Historical Survey of Jewish Diaspora (597-331 B.C.E.)

The Jewish Diaspora began with the Babylonian exile in the 6th century B.C.E. In 597, Nebuchadnezzar, king of Babylon, captured the city of Jerusalem and exiled to Babylon the royal family of Judea, the high officials, and leading citizens of the city. Then in 587, his army put a torch to the city and razed it to the ground. Certain of the ecclesiastical, military, and civil officials and leading citizens were executed, and a large portion of the population was deported to Babylon. Of those who were not forcibly exiled, many left voluntarily to seek safety elsewhere. A considerable number of them found refuge in Egypt. This catastrophe brought to an end the kingdom of Judah and was the beginning of the Jewish Diaspora, the scattering of the Jewish people among the nations. The Jewish community in Babylon soon became an important center of Diaspora life and remained so throughout the Hellenistic-Roman period. Unlike the Hellenistic Diaspora in Egypt, Asia Minor, and Europe that adopted Greek as a first language, the Babylonian exiles retained Aramaic as their primary language. This fact also helped them to continue their close contacts with the homeland, and they had a significant influence in the development of normative Judaism. Many of the Hebrew Scriptures were written or edited by the Babylonian exiles. The writings preserve the records and traditions of the past and stress the observance of the Sabbath and the ceremonial laws. After the destruction of Jerusalem in 70 C.E. and the reorganization of Judaism by the rabbis who met in Jamnia (Yavneh) in 90, it was the Babylonian text of the Hebrew Bible that was accepted as canonical, replacing the Palestinian text that had been used until then.

Nebuchadnezzar's empire was short-lived. In 539, it was conquered by the Persians. The Persian king Cyrus adopted a more lenient policy than the Babylonian king. He encouraged the Diaspora Jews to return to Jerusalem and to rebuild their temple. Some returned, but many who were now well established in Babylon preferred to remain, while others migrated to other parts of the East. Under the tolerant rule of the Persians, Jewish communities continued to flourish and to spread throughout Mesopotamia. During the Persian period, the largest portion of the Jewish population was living outside of Judea (Palestine). The largest and the wealthiest Diaspora was in Babylon, and it was this group that was influential in establishing the national and religious center of the Jewish people, although from afar. The temple of Jerusalem was rebuilt between 520 and 515, and legislation was introduced to secure Israel's semi-autonomous state and its particular religious character that emphasized religious purity and the exclusion of interfaith marriages. For the most part, Jewish life under Persian rule was relatively peaceful.

In 331, Alexander of Macedon defeated the Persian army at Gaugamela and became master of the vast Persian Empire, initiating its rapid hellenization. Greek influences had penetrated the Persian Empire, which included Judea, as early as the 6th/5th century. In the 5th century, during which Persia and Greece had constant relationships, either friendly or hostile, this influence became more extensive. Greek mercenaries, scholars, and tradesmen were found throughout the Persian realm, and Greek imports poured into Judea through Phoenician ports. By the 4th century, Jewish coins imitated Greek issues for trading with the Greeks. Even Jewish literature from this period reveals the influence of Greek ideas. However, it

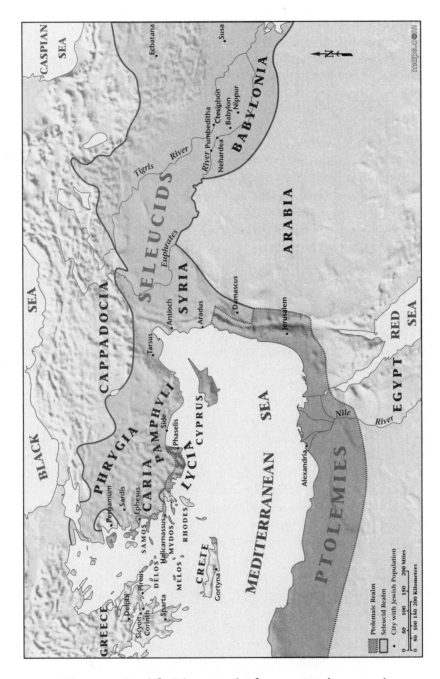

Map 3.1   Jewish Diaspora (3rd-1st centuries B.C.E.)

was not until Judea came under the rule of Alexander and his successors that the Jewish people experienced the direct, large-scale impact of Greek culture.

Alexander's aim and the effect of his conquests were to unite the East with the West, politically and culturally. He sought to bring about a fusion of ideas, Greek and oriental, in a cosmopolitan empire.[1] To this end, Alexander established cities and colonies, all focuses of Hellenism, at key areas of the empire and encouraged groups of his diverse subjects, many of which were Jews from Palestine, to migrate. He himself had many Palestinian Jews resettled in his new foundation, Alexandria, Egypt, which he designed and named after himself. The migration of Jews from their homeland to the various parts of the empire resulted in a new and extensive Jewish dispersion. The Jewish population, especially in Alexandria, increased greatly and the city soon became the most important center of world Jewry, surpassing the Babylonian community. The latter continued to be an important Jewish community of the Diaspora. Other important Jewish settlements were found throughout Asia Minor and Syria. By the end of the 1st century B.C.E., Jews living outside of Palestine outnumbered those living at home. They were dispersed over the entire Hellenistic-Roman world, with the majority living in Egypt.

Jewish contact with Hellenism inevitably led to a certain amount of assimilation and imitation. The effects of hellenization were more profound in the Diaspora than in Palestine, where the Palestinian Jews vigorously rejected all that Hellenistic culture had to offer. Their national religious consciousness resisted any major assimilation with Hellenism, and it never succeeded in undermining Palestinian Judaism. Neither did the Greek language, which had now become the lingua franca of the civilized world, ever completely replace Aramaic as the language of the people nor Hebrew as the major vehicle of literature.

B. Hellenization of the Jewish Diaspora

Information on the Jewish Diaspora is sparse, fragmentary, and often not based on accurate historical sources. The little evidence available refers mainly to the Diaspora in Egypt, and especially Alexandria. Of the other

---

1. For a discussion of Alexander's goal and effect, see the introduction above.

Diaspora communities in Asia Minor, Syria, Greece, and later in Rome, brief and isolated pieces of information are preserved in contemporary writings or on artifacts discovered in excavations. These meager sources suggest that the situation in the other Diaspora territories was comparable to that in Egypt.[2] Early accounts indicate that under the rule of the Ptolemies the Jews in Egypt enjoyed friendly relations. There were occasionally tense situations, but these were primarily political. There is no clear trace of persecution or hostility to the Jews until the time of Roman rule beginning in the late 1st century B.C.E.

As Egypt's economic and political power developed, Jewish participation increased in every sphere of activity. Prosperous military colonies existed as early as 310, and Jews were appointed to offices in the administrative and financial hierarchy of Ptolemaic Egypt. They also served as tax farmers, tax collectors, bank employees, and craftsmen. Most of the Jews who lived in the countryside and provincial towns were farmers, farm workers, herdsmen, and shepherds. Although they were not permitted citizenship,[3] the Jews enjoyed considerable privileges of their own, which in some respects gave them an advantage over the citizens. They were allowed quasi-autonomous community organizations that were headed by a chief magistrate, an ethnarch, who conducted the affairs of the community, administered justice, and supervised the implementation of contracts and ordinances. During the reign of Augustus, in the years 12-10 B.C.E, a *gerousia*, a council of elders, was substituted for the ethnarch's position. The Jewish communities were permitted to live according to their ancestral laws. This included the right to build synagogues, maintain their own courts of law according to their customs, educate their youth in the Jewish tradition, establish communal institutions, and elect their own officials. Every Jewish community in the Diaspora had its own *proseuchai*, houses of prayer, which later came to be known as synagogues.[4] Some of the earliest *proseuchai* existed in Egypt in the mid-3rd century. The *proseuchae*, or synagogue, was the center of Jewish social and religious life. It was a place of prayer, of instruction and justice, and even a hospice for Jewish travelers.[5]

2. Victor Tcherikover, *Hellenistic Civilization and the Jews* (1959, repr. New York: Athenerum, 1970), 287-95.

3. Jews in general were not permitted citizenship. However, individual Jews could acquire citizenship through special governmental permission; see Tcherikover, ch. 2.

4. The development of the synagogue is discussed in section D below.

5. Tcherikover, 303.

Although the Diaspora Jews maintained a largely autonomous political and religious existence, they also actively participated in all aspects of Hellenistic life of the territories in which they lived — political, military, civic, economic, and cultural. By the 3rd century B.C.E., during the reign of Ptolemy II Philadelphus (282-246), the Jews had become an important and influential element in Egypt. In Alexandria, the center of Hellenistic culture, was the *mouseion* and its history. Founded by Ptolemy I Soter (323-285), it promoted the study of the sciences and the liberal arts, and was similar to a modern-day institute of advanced study. It soon became the greatest single center of Hellenistic culture. The library, situated nearby, was designed to facilitate the work of the scholars in the *mouseion* and as a repository for at least one copy of every literary work available. In constant contact with the Hellenistic world, the Jewish Diaspora, especially in Alexandria, soon assimilated its language and thought. Papyri evidences indicate that by the early 3rd century the Jews of Alexandria had adopted Greek as their native tongue and attempted to adjust their religious ideas to the intellectual viewpoint of the dominant culture. The Hellenistic Jews not only spoke and wrote Greek but also prayed in Greek, sang Greek psalms, and produced Greek literature influenced by Greek thought.[6] Hence, the need arose for a Greek translation of the Hebrew Scriptures to meet the religious and educational needs of the community.

The Septuagint

The translation of the Hebrew Scriptures into Greek is the most significant literary achievement of the Hellenistic Jewish Diaspora. It is known as the Septuagint, or "Translation of the Seventy," because of the legend concerning its origin, and is often abbreviated with the Roman numerals LXX. The legend is preserved in the *Letter of Aristeas to Philocrates*,[7] in which the author poses as a Greek official at the court of Ptolemy II Philadelphus. Although called a letter, it is actually a short treatise addressed to his brother Philocrates. According to Aristeas, Demetrius of Phalerum, the renowned

6. Louis H. Feldman, *Jew and Gentile in the Ancient World* (Princeton: Princeton University Press, 1993), 51-52 and n.

7. A copy of the document in Greek with an English translation, commentary, and critical notes is found in Moses Hadas, ed., *Aristeas to Philocrates* (1951, repr. New York: Ktav, 1973).

librarian of the Alexandrian library, informed Ptolemy II that the library did not possess a copy of the Jewish Scriptures, the Torah or Pentateuch. To remedy the situation, the king wrote to the high priest in Jerusalem and requested 72 Jewish scholars, six from each of the 12 tribes, to come to Alexandria to translate the Scriptures for the library. Along with the request Ptolemy sent gifts to the Jerusalem Jews. In Egypt, to show his goodwill, he freed more than 100 thousand Jewish slaves. Ptolemy's request was granted by the high priest, and 72 scholars came to Egypt and completed the translation in 72 days. The translation was so accurately executed that it was never to be altered. Aristeas's account of the Septuagint's origin was amended and/or expanded in later years by both rabbis and Christian authors. One version claims that, through divine inspiration, all the scholars, each one working independently, produced the very same Greek text.

The account, as well as the later revisions, is legend. It is a Jewish propagandist tract written by an anonymous Jew sometime between 145 and 100 B.C.E. Most scholars accept the latter year as the probable date of composition.[8] The Letter is a eulogy of Judaism, addressed to a non-Jewish audience for the purpose of defending Judaism against its pagan critics, to glorify Judaism and its writings, and to acquaint the Greeks with the Jewish Scriptures. Although the account is largely fictitious, it does contain a kernel of historical truth. The Pentateuch or Torah was translated in Alexandria during the reign of Ptolemy II, but not by six scholars from each of the tribes or in 72 days. It is believed to have been completed ca. 250 B.C.E. Whether it was commissioned by Ptolemy is uncertain.[9] The other books of the Old Testament were gradually translated into Greek over the following two centuries but were ascribed to the original translators; Isaiah and Jeremiah, the Prophets and Psalms were added sometime between 170-132. In the late 2nd or early 1st century B.C.E. were added the Wisdom of Solomon and 3 and 4 Maccabees, which were originally written in Greek, and the so-called Apocryphal/Deuterocanonical works, works that were not included in the Hebrew canon. These include Tobit, Judith, 1 and 2 Maccabees, 1 Esdras, Ecclesiasticus (Sirach), 1 Baruch, the Letter of Jeremiah, and additions to Esther and Daniel. The last book to be added was Ecclesiastes,

8. Hadas, 17-18.

9. Most scholars believe that Ptolemy's involvement in the translation is fiction. Elias J. Bickerman, *The Jews in the Greek Age* (Cambridge, Mass.: Harvard University Press, 1988), 101-2, however accepts Aristeas's statement that the translation was done under the patronage of the king.

the extant Greek of which dates to ca. 100 C.E. The Greek collection of Old Testament writings is more inclusive than the Hebrew Bible that was determined by the rabbis in Jamnia in 90 C.E.

The Development of Apocalyptic and Wisdom Theology Literature

The translation of the Septuagint was the first literary work of the Hellenistic Jews and was of major significance. It provided the Bible for a large number of Jews who could no longer read the original Hebrew. The need for a Greek translation did not exist only in Egypt, but in other areas of the Diaspora as well as in Palestine. Extant Jewish literature from Palestine written in Greek is based on the Septuagint, and several fragments from the Qumran caves attest to the use of the Septuagint among the Palestinian Jews.[10] Moreover, the Greek Bible was the medium through which the religious experience of the Jews was communicated to the Hellenistic-Roman world. It was the main factor in the hellenization of Judaism and enabled it to become a world religion, one of the strongest and most widespread of the Hellenistic-Roman period. The Septuagint served as the basis of all subsequent Hellenistic-Jewish literature, both biblical and nonbiblical.

A translation seldom if ever conveys precisely the same concepts as the original. Some words in the original do not have exact equivalents in the language of the translation, and there are differences which the words have acquired in different contexts of thought. Thus, much of a translation is basically an interpretation. The translation of the Hebrew Torah into Greek introduced Greek concepts into Jewish thought. Although the original translators endeavored to render the text as literally as possible, Hebrew words and idioms that had no Greek equivalent or concepts that were obscure were interpreted or elucidated.[11] With Greek the language of the Bible and the synagogue and its influences on Jewish literature, the Diaspora Jews gradually began to assimilate Hellenistic ideas and concepts and attempted to understand the Scriptures under the influence of

10. W. D. Davies and Louis Finkelstein, eds., *The Cambridge History of Judaism,* 2 (Cambridge: Cambridge University Press, 1989): 386.

11. For a discussion of the Septuagint as a translation, see Elias J. Bickerman, "The Septuagint as a Translation," *Studies in Jewish and Christian History,* 1. AGJU 9/1 (Leiden: E. J. Brill, 1976): 167-200.

those ideas. They interpreted the Scriptures allegorically and discovered in them the deepest philosophical and metaphysical truths. Allegorical interpretation of the Scriptures was the distinctive literary product of Alexandrian Judaism. The master of this interpretation and the principal figure of Hellenistic-Jewish philosophy is Philo Judaeus (ca. 20 B.C.E.-50 C.E.).[12] Allegorical interpretation of the Bible was also conducted in the Palestinian schools, but the dangers of its excessive use were soon recognized and its progress was checked. The emphasis in these schools continued to be the literal sense of the Hebraic tradition. By means of allegory, the Creation story is understood as a cosmogony and described according to Greek cosmogonic concepts. The religious rites and the Sabbath, although they continued to be observed in the traditional ancestral way, were understood symbolically. Much of the Jewish literary output in Greek during the 3rd and 2nd centuries B.C.E. interpreted the whole of the Mosaic law as a code of rational ethics. It deliberately adopted Greek ideas in support of Judaism as a philosophical religion in harmony with the Hellenistic intellectual environment. Of special significance in the Jewish world of the times was the development of apocalyptic literature and the later wisdom literature, which produced a fundamental change in the theological thought of Israel.

The origins of apocalypticism can be traced to the dualism of Zoroastrianism, the ancient religion of Persia. Influenced by Hellenism, it developed into a distinctive Jewish literary genre during the late 3rd to early 2nd centuries B.C.E. Although apocalyptic elements are found in earlier biblical writings, primarily Ezekiel and Second Isaiah, they are closer in content and form to the prophetic writings of the Old Testament.[13] Jewish apocalyptic literature flourished and enjoyed an enormous popularity both within Palestine and the Diaspora between 200 B.C.E. and 90 C.E. This literature replaced the writings of the prophetic age, which had come to an end. The apocalypticists continued the tradition of the prophets by adopting the major themes of the prophetic teachings, in particular the prediction element, and incorporated them into a novel world-historical, cosmic form. Many apocalyptic works were written during times of hardship and oppression. These conditions were depicted by the writers in a cosmic set-

---

12. The works of Philo are discussed below in section C.

13. Martin Hengel, *Judaism and Hellenism: Studies in their Encounter in Palestine during the Early Hellenistic Period* (Philadelphia: Fortress, 1974) 1:180-81.

ting, perceived not only as a local or national situation but one of universal significance, and accompanied by supernatural signs. Apocalyptic literature does not lend itself to a systematic description. It is not a homogeneous corpus and varies in form, emphasis, and in the presentation of the message. Nonetheless, certain common characteristics are found in the majority of the works.[14]

The term "apocalyptic" is a Greek noun, *apokalypsis,* meaning a revelation, a disclosure, a vision. Apocalyptic writings purport to be divine revelations in the form of a series of dreams or visions that were disclosed to a noted biblical sage, from Adam to Ezra, and interpreted by an angel.[15] The literary device of pseudonymity is ascribed to the works to give credence to the author's message. In mysterious and enigmatic language, they reveal the divine secrets of human destiny and the last events, which were thought to be impending imminently. Apocalypticists divide history, the time of this world, into a series of epochs or ages, usually four, but sometimes seven, 10, or 12. History was periodized to emphasize that the events of human history were predetermined by God from the days of creation, and to establish for the reader his/her position in the divinely ordained time scheme. Mythical images rich in symbolism are used to describe persons, nations, and events in history. Individuals and nations are represented as various birds or beasts, sometimes bizarre, and historical events as natural occurrences. In some works, numerology is used to calculate the exact time of the end, which was soon to come. Much of this material was derived from concepts of the Hellenistic oriental environment.

Apocalypticists often present a pessimistic view of the world with a marked tendency towards dualism. According to them, this world is evil and, unlike the Old Testament prophets, who believed that the world is under God's control and improvable, they believe the present age is irretrievable. Although God controls the world and its history, the world has been led astray by Satan and the fallen angels, the demons. All of history's struggles are a reflection of the cosmic struggle between God and the evil powers, which hold the world in their evil grasp. However, God will soon inter-

---

14. For a discussion of the diversity among apocalyptic writers, see D. S. Russell, *The Method and Message of Jewish Apocalyptic, 200 BC–AD 100.* OTL (Philadelphia: Westminster, 1964), ch. VIII.

15. Angels in the apocalyptic writings serve as messengers of God or mediators between God and human beings. A few apocalypses have a developed angelology and demonology, with angels on God's side in the cosmic drama and demons on the side of evil.

vene and engage them in a cosmic conflict in which the whole of creation will be involved. The last days are described as a time of great trouble, the worst the world has ever seen. Some apocalypses predict vast terrestrial disasters and cosmic disturbances. After the cosmic drama during which Satan and the evil powers will be destroyed, there will follow a universal resurrection and judgment. All who had died will be resurrected and will be judged along with the living. Many apocalypses view the resurrection as spiritual rather than physical. In the final judgment, all creation, visible and invisible, all nations, all departed souls now raised from the dead, the angels, and the demons will be judged according to their righteous or evil deeds. The righteous will live under the rule of God in eternal bliss and the wicked in eternal punishment. Judgment, according to most apocalypses, will be pronounced by God sitting on his throne. In some, however, God acts through his agent, a transcendent being referred to as Son of Man or Messiah, an anointed or chosen one. Following the Judgment, God will inaugurate a new age under his sovereignty. This new world or kingdom is understood in some works as an earthly one; others consider it a heavenly kingdom. Written during times of hardship and oppression, the apocalyptic writings were a source of encouragement and strength to the pious facing dire peril and danger. They also served as a warning to sinners and to those who had become lax in their faith to repent while there was still time.

Numerous apocalypses were written between the 2nd century B.C.E. and the 1st century C.E. They were written in Hebrew, Aramaic, and Greek in both Palestine and the Diaspora. Examples of apocalyptic material were also found among the Qumran or Dead Sea Scrolls. Their large number and widespread distribution is an indication of their popularity and significance to the Jewish people as a whole. In the Diaspora, especially Alexandria, they gained greater influence and popularity than in Palestine. They were widely circulated, and in due course were translated into the various languages of the Diaspora — Syriac, Arabic, Armenian, Ethiopic, Slavonic, Georgian, and Latin. By the 2nd century C.E., however, the popularity of the writings began to wane. Much of their decline is due to the reaction of the rabbis who met in Jamnia (Yavneh) in 90 C.E. to restructure Judaism after the destruction of the temple and of Jerusalem. They considered certain features of the writings influenced by Hellenistic and other foreign elements and thus unacceptable to reformed Judaism. In particular, they disagreed with the dualistic view of the cosmos and the human sphere, the developed eschatology with its emphasis on life after death, its rewards and punishments, and the immortality of the soul. These concepts were of little concern in the religion of ancient Israel or reformed Judaism with its strict devotion to the law and the Scriptures. They were Hellenistic beliefs shared by many of the cults and religions of the age. As a result, apocalyptic literature was no longer written or used, either in Palestine or in the Diaspora, and in time many were lost. None of the canonical works written in Hebrew or Aramaic, except the book of Daniel, survive in their original form or language but in translation in other languages, especially Greek. The extant writings are a small fraction of what at one time was a very considerable literature. They represent the books most highly valued by the Christians, who by the 1st century had adopted and adapted many of the Jewish apocalypses. The adoption of these works by the Christians was also a strong factor in the decline of apocalypticism among mainstream Judaism.[16]

Early Christianity's adoption and adaptation of the existing Jewish apocalypses has made it difficult for scholars to determine the date or origin of a number of the works. Moreover, they are not all true apocalypses, but merely contain certain apocalyptic elements. Thus, there is no generally accepted grouping of the writings.[17] Two of the most significant and undisputed examples of apocalyptic literature of the period are the book of Daniel and the book of Enoch. Daniel is among the earliest "historical" apocalypses and, over time, one of the most influential for later works in that genre, both Jewish and Christian, having the distinction of being the only complete apocalypse to be included in the Hebrew Old Testament canon. The reason for its acceptance into the canon is that it is attributed to an early prominent religious authority.[18] Although attributed to a Jewish sage at the court of the 6th-century Babylonian king Nebuchadnezzar, the book in its final form is a product of the Maccabean struggle during the reign of Antiochus IV Epiphanes (168-164). It is considered to have been written ca. 165 B.C.E., and is written partly in Hebrew and partly in Aramaic. In true apocalyptic fashion, the work recounts, in the form of

16. Russell, 32.

17. For a list of texts that are considered apocalyptic or comprise apocalyptic elements, see Russell, 37. An extensive bibliography for each writing is found in Emil Schürer, *The History of the Jewish People in the Age of Jesus Christ: 175 B.C.–A.D. 135*, rev. ed. (Edinburgh: T. & T. Clark, 1986), 3/1-2.

18. Schürer, 3/1: 247.

prophecy, the events of history up to the time of the writing. The importance of Daniel is its development of the doctrine of the general resurrection, the rewards and punishments of the afterlife, and the triumph and establishment of God's rule (Dan. 12:1-3). Daniel is also the first to interpret the Old Testament phrase "son of man" and to give it a specific identity. The phrase as used in the Old Testament merely means "human being," or collectively "human beings." In Daniel, it can be interpreted as a corporate figure who represents all the faithful of God, those presently living as well as those who are now dead and will be resurrected at the final judgment (Dan. 7:9-18). It is these individuals who, in a corporate sense, will preside in God's new earthly kingdom, an everlasting kingdom devoid of all evil. Daniel's importance during the Hellenistic-Roman period is evident from allusions to the work only a few decades after its composition — in the oldest Sibylline Oracles ca. 150 B.C.E., 1 Maccabees ca. 100, and the first part of 1 Baruch ca. 150-125, as well as from the large number of fragments of the work that were found in the Qumran caves. The Qumran finds contain the earliest extant manuscripts of Daniel, and one is considered to belong to the late 2nd century.[19]

Next to Daniel, the book of Enoch or 1 Enoch is the most important apocalypse of the period under discussion. It is a composite of five major sections written by various authors and edited in its final form between 164 and 63 B.C.E. It was originally written in Aramaic, but is extant in its entirety only in Ethiopic, which itself is a translation from a Greek version of which only a part has survived. Aramaic fragments of the work were recently found among the Qumran scrolls. The extant Ethiopic version dates from the 1st-2nd centuries C.E. 1 Enoch had more influence on the writing of the New Testament and on the early church fathers than any other noncanonical apocalyptic literature. It is quoted in the New Testament Epistle of Jude (Jude 14-15), and a number of phrases in other New Testament writings are dependent on the work.[20] The writing was accepted and used by many church fathers as a genuine work of the Hebrew patriarch Enoch. 1 Enoch purports to be a series of divine revelations that were disclosed to Enoch in a dream, and they encompass the laws of nature, the history of the world from Adam to the final judgment and the establish-

19. Schürer, 3/1: 248.

20. James D. Newsome, *Greeks, Romans, Jews: Currents of Culture and Belief in the New Testament World* (Philadelphia: Trinity, 1992), 84-85.

ment of God's kingdom. Of considerable importance, especially for early Christianity, is the second section of the work known as the Similitudes or Parables of Enoch (chs. 37–71) with its eschatological emphasis on the preexistent messiah, the resurrection of the dead, and the last judgment. In 1 Enoch, the preexistent messiah is the Son of Man, also called the Elect One, and he assumes a greater significance than in the book of Daniel. He is described as a preexistent, supernatural divine being, the representative of the living God. In the final judgment, the Son of Man will preside along with God as judge of all, men and angels, the living and the dead, who will be resurrected and judged along with the living. The righteous, those living and those resurrected, will live in eternal bliss in God's kingdom that will be ruled by the Son of Man, while the wicked will suffer eternal torments. As in the book of Daniel, God's kingdom in 1 Enoch is an earthly kingdom. In Enoch, the center of the kingdom is the city of Jerusalem, a new city established by God to replace the old city and its original site (chs. 6–36; 90:30-31). Much of the New Testament's language concerning Jesus was influenced by the concept of the Son of Man and the titles conferred upon him in the Similitudes of 1 Enoch.

Apocalypticism was Judaism's response to the Jewish concerns of the time, the significance of the individual's life in the presence of the divine will, and his/her salvation and destiny — concerns shared by many during the Hellenistic-Roman period. Its literature was one of hope and its emphasis the future hope, not only of the nation of Israel that was stressed in the Old Testament prophetic hope, but also of the individual who will share in God's kingdom by means of resurrection. Moreover, the message of apocalypticism is universal; it is not limited to any one nation or people. God's salvation extends to all the righteous, and his judgments will fall upon all the wicked. Similar to the contemporary cults and religions, Jewish apocalypticists adopted and adapted the prevalent elements of Hellenistic cosmology and its view of human destiny. These they incorporated into the traditional Jewish beliefs to reveal a deeper understanding of the only true and living God. Closely associated with the rise of apocalypticism and its understanding of the cosmos and human destiny was the development of the literature of wisdom theology. Principal of these works during this period were Qoheleth (ca. 270-220 B.C.E.), the Wisdom of Ben Sirach (ca. 180), referred to in the Septuagint as Ecclesiastes and Ecclesiasticus respectively, and the Wisdom of Solomon (ca. 100-50).

Wisdom is international, and wisdom traditions existed in Israel as well as among many other cultures of antiquity. In ancient Near East cultures, wisdom represented an effort to understand the order in the natural and human world empirically and to collect these experiences and transmit them as doctrine. Early Israelite wisdom reflects the approach of its common Near Eastern heritage. It is a rational reflective way of dealing with human existence. The term "wisdom," *hokmah,* in early biblical literature is used to mean practical good sense, the ability to live life intelligently, virtuously, and successfully. In time, it became a synonym for the Law, the Torah.[21] After the Babylonian conquest and the collapse of Israel's social and political structure, wisdom came to be viewed in a new way. Influenced by foreign thought and the need for a deeper understanding of the world, life's purpose, and human destiny, wisdom was perceived not only as an attribute of the wise or even of God himself, but as having an independent existence. It developed from practical wisdom, daily prudence verifiable in experience, to theological wisdom, a transcendent cosmic principle of order. As such, wisdom had an independent, personal existence and was frequently personified and on occasion hypostatized.[22] Wisdom is described as a divine agent, the first creation of God through whom all things were brought into being and are sustained.[23] The speculation about hypostatized wisdom, which began after the Babylonian exile, was further developed during the Hellenistic period and was influenced by the social and political conditions of the time and the prevailing concepts.

In the Jewish literature of the Hellenistic period, Wisdom is not only a companion of God at creation but a universal power that pervades the whole world. In Ben Sirach (Ecclesiasticus) and the Wisdom of Solomon, Wisdom is a world reason that emanates from God and existed before all creation. She[24] permeates the whole of creation, all of nature and humanity, and it is because of her that mankind is a rational being.[25] Wisdom instructs humanity about its divine origin and destiny.[26] The wise are those who choose to follow her instructions. They understand their divine ori-

---

21. This identification is expressed frequently throughout the Old Testament. See esp. Deut. 4:6; Ezra 7:25; Ps. 37:30ff.; 111:10; 112:1; 119:97-104.

22. Cf. Prov. 8:22–9:1; Job 28.

23. Prov. 3:19; 8:22-31; Job 28:25-27.

24. The term "wisdom," *hokmah* in Hebrew and *sophia* in Greek, is feminine, and thus translated as "she."

25. Sir. 1:4-10, 14-19; 24:1-6; Wis. 7:22-27; 8:1.

26. Sir. 4:11-19; Wis. 7:15-20.

gin and destiny and the true course of the world. They live a virtuous and successful life and are guided by wisdom to final justification and vindication.[27] In Ben Sirach, wisdom's instructions are identical to the teachings and demands of the Torah.[28] The predicates of personified divine wisdom in Ben Sirach and the Wisdom of Solomon are similar to the descriptions of the qualities of the Hellenistic goddess Isis found in her aretalogies.[29] This is an indication of Isis's widespread influence and importance. The speculative and personal features of divine wisdom were further developed by the Hellenistic Jews, especially of Alexandria, and had an affinity to similar Greek concepts.

The optimistic wisdom theology found in Ben Sirach and the Wisdom of Solomon was not shared by all Jewish wisdom writers. A skeptical Palestinian wisdom best expressed in Qoheleth (Ecclesiastes) presents a pessimistic view of God, the world, and human destiny. This view rejects the concept of a divine destiny for humans, life after death, and the importance of wisdom in human existence that is emphasized in the optimistic wisdom literature of the time. In Qoheleth, human existence as well as the existence of the world itself are marked by a cycle of coming into being and passing away, without any novelty or progress. The present is like the past, there is nothing new under the sun, and everyone will soon die (Eccl. 1:5-11). Thus, nothing has any meaning; everything is only "vanity and a chasing after wind" (1:2, 14; 12:8), even the search for truth and wisdom. Truth is unattainable, for human beings are incapable of understanding the mysteries of the world, human existence, or the way God governs the universe; and wisdom, when it is sought, produces only misery (1:12-18; 8:16-17). Moreover, the evils of society reveal that there is no discernible difference between the fate of the righteous and that of the wicked, and one cannot be certain of a just retribution in the hereafter (3:16–4:3; 9:1-2). Therefore, the author repeatedly stresses that what remains for an individual is to find enjoyment in life and work during the brief span of the vain life allotted to everyone, since there is nothing after death.[30] The pursuit of happiness is God's great commandment for mankind (2:24-26; 9:7-10). Life is to be lived to its fullest, but in moderation. An individual should avoid all ex-

27. Sir. 6:18-22, 24-29; 24:19-22; Wis. 6:17-20; 8:7-18; 10:9-10.

28. Sir. 24:8-9, 23-29.

29. Esp. Sir. 24; Wis. 7:1-8. For Isis, see above, pp. 26-30 and nn.

30. The emphasis on the enjoyment of life is found in almost every chapter. See esp. 2:1-3, 24; 3:12-13, 22; 5:18-19; 9:7-12.

tremes, whether of goodness or of wickedness (7:15-22), and always be mindful of the Creator and resign oneself to the world that God made and the rules he established for it. As the creator of all, God knows the meaning of everything that happens, even though humans do not, and is the judge of all (3:14-15; 5:1-6; 11:5-10).

Qoheleth's view presents an alternative answer to the Jewish concerns of the time. Its message is one of acceptance and enjoyment of life. Since, as Qoheleth asserts, everything in life is only vanity and there is nothing after death, the best that an individual can do is to accept what life offers and enjoy the little day-to-day pleasures: fine foods, wine, clothing, a loving spouse, and gratification in one's work. These enjoyments, although empty like life itself, do provide something — they make life endurable. The skeptical view of Qoheleth was not that typical of Jewish Hellenism. It was wisdom theology and its identification with the Torah and its affinity to the Hellenistic view of the world and human existence that was further developed and came to full fruition in the thought of Philo of Alexandria.

C. Philo of Alexandria

Philo Judaeus or Alexandrinus, more commonly known as Philo of Alexandria, was a product of the Greek-speaking Jewish Hellenistic community of Alexandria and one of the most significant representatives and the most prolific author of Hellenistic Judaism. His work is mainly a correlation of biblical revelation and Greek philosophy. To bring the Scriptures into conformity with Greek philosophical thought, Philo employs the popular method of his time, that of allegorical interpretation. Interpreting the Scriptures allegorically, and primarily the Pentateuch, he was successful in reconciling Hebrew theology with Greek philosophy, while preserving intact the observance of the law. Philo was not the first to use the method of allegory nor the first to attempt a synthesis of Greek and Hebrew thought. Allegorical interpretation had been practiced by the Greek exegetes of Homer from the end of the 6th century and later systematized by the Stoics. The purpose was to reinterpret the mythological tales of the Homeric gods and to bring them into conformity with contemporary philosophical convictions. In the Hellenistic age, the allegorical method was especially popular in Alexandria and was used by pagans and Jews and later Christians. Among the Hellenistic Jews, the 2nd-century Alexandrian philosopher Aristobulus was the first to apply the allegorical method to the interpretation of the Pentateuch, and the first to attempt to reconcile Greek and Hebrew thought. Although his work is extant only in five fragments preserved by the church historian Eusebius of Caesarea (ca. 260-340 c.e.) and is also cited, but less accurately, by Clement of Alexandria (ca. 150-ca. 215), certain important aspects of Aristobulus's thought are discernible.

According to the scanty fragments, Aristobulus's concern was the theological/philosophical interpretation of the Mosaic law.[31] The work is addressed to "King Ptolemy," considered to be Ptolemy VI Philometer (180-145). By means of allegory and metaphor, which Aristobulus asserts is the correct way of understanding the law, he states that the anthropomorphic descriptions of God found in the Scriptures refer to God's power and the permanence of the world and its laws.[32] Aristobulus was also successful in finding in the law the tenets of Greek philosophy and concluded that if the Scriptures, correctly interpreted, reveal the principles of Greek thought, then it must be assumed that the Greek philosophers and poets borrowed from Moses, the giver of the law.[33] In his allegorical interpretation of Genesis, Aristobulus is the first to identify Jewish divine wisdom with the Hellenistic philosophical idea of the Logos that created the world, permeates and orders it, and to which mankind owes its knowledge of human and divine matters.[34] The Alexandrian Jewish religious philosophy and the allegorical interpretation of the Scriptures on which it is based that was developed by Aristobulus reached their culmination and end in the works of Philo. After the fall of the temple in 70 c.e., they were rejected by Judaism and were superseded by the rabbinical tradition. Philo represents the first major blend of Judaism and Hellenism, and its climax. Employing the allegorical method of interpreting the Bible, and adopting and adapting the ideas of the eclectic Platonism of the time that included many of the ideas of Aristotle, the Stoics, and Neo-Pythagoreans, Philo developed a unique Jewish Hellenistic means of salvation through a knowledge and understanding of the origin and nature of the universe and of mankind. His thought was intended for all, Jew and pa-

31. The fragments of Aristobulus used in the study are from James H. Charlworth, ed. *The Old Testament Pseudepigrapha*, 2 (New York: Doubleday, 1985): 831-42.

32. Frag. 2.

33. Frag. 3 and 4.

34. Frag. 4:1-5; 5.

gan, since, according to Philo, the principal texts of Greek philosophy are also found in the Mosaic law.

Philo's[35] thought begins with the idea of God and concludes with the demand for union with him. God, according to Philo, is pure Being, the One or Monad, an indivisible unity, a single, uncreated, uncompounded nature, incorporeal, occupying no space or place, incorruptible, immutable, and eternal.[36] He is absolutely transcendent, beyond the Good and the Beautiful.[37] As such, God is devoid of all qualities and cannot be placed in any categories in which finite beings are classified.[38] Thus, God's nature is beyond definition. All that can be said is that God *is,* not *what* God is.[39] Perfect and transcendent, God cannot come into direct contact with matter; an intermediary being was necessary. This entity is the Logos. The Logos is the divine reason, the instrument of God's activity and his immanent manifestation in the universe. Philo's concept of the Logos is imprecise and often inconsistent. It is understood to have three main stages of existence. First, it exists as the mind or thought of God, existing from all eternity.[40] Second, the Logos exists as an incorporeal being generated or begotten by God prior to the creation of the cosmos, capable of being conceived apart from God as an encasement of the whole of his ideas (i.e., as the whole of the intelligible universe, the world of concepts or ideas), and used as an instrument or pattern in the creation of the visible world. In its second stage, the Logos corresponds to the Platonic World of Forms and is called by Philo "the idea of ideas," the first-begotten son of the uncreated Father, "the image of God,"[41] the oldest and most all embracing of all things that have come into existence,[42] not uncreated like God, nor created as mankind, but in the midst between two extremes.[43] After the creation of the material world, the Logos entered its third stage. It became immanent

35. The works of Philo used in this study are from *Philo,* ed. and trans. by F. H. Colson, G. H. Whitaker, and R. Marcus. Loeb Classical Library. 12 vols. (New York: Putnam, 1929-1962). A more detailed discussion of Philo's thought is found in Antonía Tripolitis, *The Doctrine of the Soul,* 5-16 and nn., 37-42.

36. *Leg.* 1.15.51; 2.1.2ff.; *Conf.* 27.136.
37. *Opif.* 2.8; *Leg.* 2.1.2ff.
38. *Leg.* 1.15.51.
39. *Leg.* 3.73.206.
40. *Opif.* 4.19ff.
41. *Migr.* 18.103; *Post.* 18.63; *Conf.* 14.63, 28.147.
42. *Leg.* 3.61.175.
43. *Her.* 42.206.

in the world, and acts as an instrument of divine providence through which the world is held in a continuous state of existence.[44] The Logos is also the intermediary between God and the world. He stands on the confines of the two and separates God and creation, being at the same time both their bond and their separation, both a suppliant with God on behalf of all human beings and God's ambassador who brings the commands of the Ruler.[45] In this third state, the Logos serves as the soul of the world with the world as its garment,[46] although Philo never calls the Logos world soul. Philo's Logos encompasses the attributes and functions of the divine triad of later Platonism and is considered an early stage in the development of this concept.

The material universe is a copy of the intelligible universe fashioned by God and dependent upon his Logos for its existence. Its creation is considered by Philo as an overflow of God's goodness, by which God remains unaffected and undiminished like the sun giving out its rays, like a torch from which all other torches are lit.[47] God bestows his goodness and benefits to all created beings in accordance with the recipient's capacities.[48] Philo conceives of the world as a great chain of being, a succession of grades of being descending from unity to plurality, from the immaterial, unchangeable, spiritual, and perfect to the material, changeable, sensible, and imperfect,[49] all of which is held together in perfect harmony by the immanent Logos.[50] The world consists of three main classes of living beings: entities that possess a soul, incorporeal souls; animals which include fishes, birds, and land animals; and human beings. The incorporeal souls are pure, rational, incorruptible immortal beings that inhabit the upper regions of the universe, the air.[51] These pure souls or minds are what philosophers call daemons or spirits and what Scripture calls angels or messengers.[52] They act as messengers of God and intermediaries between God and the human race. The animals possess only an irrational soul or principle of life and are in-

44. *Sacr.* 8.40; *Plant.* 2.9-10.
45. *Her.* 42.05-6.
46. *Fug.* 20.110.
47. *Gig.* 6.24ff.; *QG* 2.40; *Plant.* 20.89.
48. *Opif.* 6.23.
49. *Opif.* 49.141ff.; *QE* 2.68; *Immut.* 7.35.
50. *Fug.* 20.12; *Plant.* 2.9ff.
51. *Opif.* 24.73; *Conf.* 35.176; *Somn.* 1.22.137ff.; *Gig.* 2.6.
52. *Somn.* 1.22.141ff.; *Gig.* 2.6.

capable of either good or evil.[53] Human beings, the third group of living beings, combine within themselves the natures of the other two.

According to Philo, humans are of a composite nature of animal or body and soul, generally called mind.[54] The soul is composed of two parts or powers, a rational and an irrational.[55] In its original state, the rational soul was a pure being, one of the so-called angels that was attracted by the things of the earth and descended into a human body.[56] The rational soul was made by God himself in his image, using the divine Logos as a pattern, and thus is a copy, an impression of the Logos. As such, it is akin to the divine essence and is allied with God, capable of knowing and loving him.[57] Like its archetype, the Logos, the rational soul or mind is incorporeal, incorruptible, immortal, invisible, indivisible, divine, and eternal, neither male nor female.[58] It is the true being within an individual, the most supreme and best part, and thus the governing part.[59] The mind possesses many powers, among the most important of which is reasoning.[60] Concerning the irrational part of the soul, Philo claims that it was formed or molded when God created mankind out of matter.[61] It is considered the lower or inferior part of the soul because it is the seat of the passions and other irrational emotions and thus prone to evil. Being inferior, the irrational soul and the body, which acts as its tool, were not created directly by God but by the subordinate powers associated with God at creation. These powers formed the irrational part of mankind by imitating God's skill when he formed the rational part. Thus, the irrational part is an imitation or an imperfect copy of the rational part.[62] To the irrational part Philo attributes seven faculties, the five senses — sight, hearing, taste, smell, and touch — the organ of speech, and the power of reproduction. He considers sight as the best of all the irrational powers, for it has led mankind to ob-

53. *Opif.* 24.73ff.; *Conf.* 35.177.
54. *Det.* 22.82ff.; *Opif.* 46.135; *Leg.* 3.55.161.
55. *Leg.* 2.1.2; *Conf.* 35.177ff.; *Opif.* 24.73 etc.
56. *Plant.* 4.14; *Conf.* 17.77ff.; *Somn.* 1.22.138ff.
57. *Opif.* 51.145ff.; *Mut.* 39.223; *Spec.* 4.24.123; *Somn.* 1.6.34; *Det.* 22.81ff., 24.90; *Leg.* 3.51.161.
58. *Opif.* 22.67; 23.69; 46.134; *Immut.* 10.46; *Her.* 48.232.
59. *Conf.* 18.97; *Det.* 8.22; *Somn.* 1.37.215.
60. *Opif.* 22.67.
61. *Leg.* 1.12.31.
62. *Opif.* 24.74ff.; *Fug.* 13.66ff.; *Conf.* 35.179.

serve their environment. This observation has led humans to question and investigate further, resulting in the development of philosophy and a better understanding of God.[63]

There exists a reciprocal relationship between the rational and irrational parts of the soul, between the mind and the senses. The senses nourish the mind with the necessary data to understand the corporeal and incorporeal things by impressing it, as a seal on wax, with the image of material things through which the mind comprehends the visible universe.[64] Then, by evaluating the data, the mind moves beyond what is capable of being apprehended by the senses to what is perceptible only by the intellect — the world of archetypes and ideas.[65] Similarly, the senses are dependent upon the mind for their strength and operation. Without the mind, the senses would be paralyzed.[66] As the seat of reason, the mind rules over the powers of the irrational soul, governing and unifying them.[67] The irrational part, however, composed of matter, is wild and chaotic and not readily subdued by the mind. With the body as its tool, it consistently battles against reason and attempts to overpower the mind.[68] The outcome of the struggle depends on the choice made by the mind, which possesses the knowledge of good and evil and is endowed with the power of free will by which it is able to choose between right and wrong. It is with regard to this power that an individual especially resembles God.[69] Possessing a knowledge of good and evil and the power of free choice, an individual is responsible to select the good.[70] An individual is totally responsible for the choice of evil, which, according to Philo, is caused when the mind has lost control over the senses.[71] In his choice of the good, however, the individual is provided with divine grace. It cannot be attained completely on one's own. With the freedom of choice, one can only take the initial step toward the good, but he needs God's aid to attain it.[72]

---

63. *Opif.* 17.53ff.
64. *Somn.* 1.32.187-88; *Immut.* 9.42-43; *Plant.* 32.133.
65. *Somn.* 1.5.27; 32.188; *Leg.* 2.2.5-6; 3.32.97ff.
66. *Det.* 46.168ff.
67. *Migr.* 31.170.
68. *Leg.* 2.4.10; 3.22.69; *Mut.* 34.185.
69. *Immut.* 10.47-49.
70. *Immut.* 10.50.
71. *Leg.* 3.21.67ff.; 3.52.151–53.159; *Migr.* 2.7ff.
72. *Leg.* 3.46.133-37; 76.214ff.; 34.104-5; 2.13.46-47; *Ebr.* 36.144-45.

Philo insists that it is an individual's responsibility to liberate himself from the power and bonds of the senses with their tool, the body, and return to his source, the world of ideas, and to assimilation with God. To obtain this state, one must subdue the senses to the point where they are entirely passive to the prompting of reason, i.e., to live according to reason. To live according to reason is to live according to God, i.e., to have faith or trust in God, obey his commands, and maintain his law.[73] This leads an individual to true self-knowledge — the realization that all that is human is fleeting, weak, and unreal, that only the intelligibles are real and one is totally dependent on God. An individual's achievements and successes over the things of sense, and every one of his virtues, are achieved by the aid or grace of God.[74] With the attainment of self-knowledge, one is able, with God's aid, to rise above the things of sense and their distractions to master the cardinal virtues, and to begin to gain knowledge of God — of him who truly is.[75] As an individual advances toward God, he is continuously aided by God in his acquisition of true knowledge in accordance with his capability and spiritual development.[76] In the early stages of development, an individual is aided by the angels, God's ministers, and then by the Archangel, the Logos. One's spiritual progress, however, is not continuous. It is like a staircase on which the soul is at one moment ascending and at another moment returning in the opposite direction, until by God's grace he is able to subdue completely the pull of the senses.[77] Finally, led by love and longing for God, the individual arrives at a state of complete humility, receptivity, and passivity. He has passed beyond all mediacy, beyond the body, the senses, the illusion of speech and thought, beyond the rational mind or reason, and even beyond the Logos.[78] At this stage, the soul or mind of an individual has arrived at a state of ecstasy, a state in which the mind has departed from itself, has lost all consciousness of itself and the world, and is divinely inspired and possessed by God.[79] In this state, the mind has not become one or identical with God, but has been joined to God in a continuous and

73. *Abr.* 46.268ff.; *Migr.* 9.44.

74. *Leg.* 1.15.48ff.; 3.9.29ff.; 46.136ff.

75. *Plant.* 22.98; *Leg.* 1.27.86–28.89; *Somn.* 1.10.60.

76. *Mut.* 3.18ff.; *Abr.* 24.119ff.; *Spec.* 1.8.41ff.; *Opif.* 6.23.

77. *Somn.* 1.23.150-52.

78. *Leg.* 3.13.41, 62.177-78; *Opif.* 23.70; *Gig.* 11.52–13.61; *Conf.* 28.144; *Abr.* 24.121ff.; *Her.* 14.68–16.85.

79. *QG* 3.9; *Her.* 53.264-65.

unbroken union of harmony and love.[80] A soul or mind can arrive at the mystical union and direct vision of God even in this life. It had been attained by Moses, Abraham, and the prophets of the Old Testament when they spoke God's word and revealed his laws and commandments.[81] However, while in the body, it is difficult for an individual to attain to the divine vision and then only for a brief period.[82] At the death of the body, the souls that had freed themselves from the bonds of the body return to their original bodiless condition and to their native abode, the ethereal region which Philo calls the heavens. Of the souls that ascend to the heavens, some long for the material world and descend again into human bodies to repeat the cycle again.[83] The souls that lived completely in and for the body during their stay on earth are banished by God to the recesses of the underworld. There they endure continuous and unrelieved misery and torture forever.[84] What Philo means is that the unrighteous soul suffers the torments of conscience in this life — the loss of hope, feelings of gloom, grief, and continuous fear resulting from the knowledge of its evil deeds and the anguish of its anticipated punishment — as well as the punishment for its sins after death.[85]

Philo's thought, although bitterly disapproved of and finally rejected by Palestinian Jewish theologians, had a considerable influence on the development of the philosophical thought of both pagans and Christians who came after him. It was found useful by the pagan philosophers of the 2nd and 3rd centuries C.E. and greatly influenced Christian thinkers. Traces of Philo's thought are found in the New Testament, and almost all Greek-speaking theologians from the apologists to the later great church fathers drew from his thought to some degree. Philo's thought profoundly influenced the development of the Christian worldview and the concept of the individual. Although Philo had assimilated much from Hellenism, he remained a devout, practicing Jew and a loyal advocate of synagogue Judaism, which by the time of Philo was the center of all aspects of Jewish life.[86]

80. *Post.* 4.12; *Somn.* 2.34.232ff.; *Fug.* 11.58; 17.19ff.; *QE* 2.29.
81. *Mos.* 2.35.188ff.; *QG* 3.9; *Her.* 14.69, 52.258ff.; *Migr.* 15.84ff.; *Virt.* 39.217.
82. *Immut.* 1.2ff.; *Gig.* 5.19ff., 7.28ff.; 14.62ff.
83. *Somn.* 1.22.139.
84. *Cher.* 1.2ff.; *Det.* 40.147ff.; *Praem.* 26.152.
85. *Cong.* 11.57; *Praem.* 12.67-73; *Somn.* 1.23.151; *Her.* 9.45.
86. In 40 C.E., at an advanced age, Philo led a five-man delegation to the Roman emperor Gaius (Caligula) to protest against the desecration of the synagogues and the attacks

D. The Development of the Synagogue

The word "synagogue" is Greek and means simply a bringing together or a gathering, devoid of any religious connotation. It became Jewish by association during the Hellenistic-Roman period. Initially, the word was used to refer to an assembly or gathering of Jewish people for religious or socio-political purposes. By the 1st century C.E., it also came to mean the place of assembly, the edifice built for particular functions. The origin of the synagogue is unknown. Most scholars surmise that it had its beginnings during the Babylonian exile in the spontaneous gatherings of the exiled Jews in Babylonia and elsewhere to observe the Sabbath, the feasts, or fast days, to read the words of the prophets, and to pray. After the exile and the restoration of the Jerusalem temple, the Jews, and especially those in the Diaspora, continued the custom of assembly. These gatherings or assemblies did not meet in a specific physical setting, but in different places, any one of which was called the house of the assembly.[87] The earliest evidence of a distinct building for religious purposes comes from Egypt and dates from the 3rd century B.C.E. during the reign of Ptolemy III Euergetes (246-221). An extant inscription attests that the Ptolemaic kings granted to many synagogues the same asylum as was granted to the Egyptian temples, and in return, Jews dedicated their synagogues to the king and his family.[88] Two epigraphical evidences of this kind exist from the Ptolemaic period.[89] The earliest evidence of a synagogue building in Palestine is found in the Theodotus inscription discovered in Jerusalem, dating to the beginning of the 1st century C.E.[90] By the mid-1st century C.E., synagogues flourished throughout the Hellenistic-Roman world. They existed virtually in every Jewish community in Palestine and the Diaspora and, even before the destruction of the temple in 70 C.E., had become the central institution in Jewish life.

---

on the beliefs and practices of its assemblies. These are described in his treatise *Legatio ad Gaium* and referred to in *In Flaccum*. See esp. *Legat.* 16.114-19; 17.120-31; 20.132-36; *Flacc.* 6.41-42; 7.53-55.

87. Solomon Zeitlin, "The Origin of the Synagogue," *American Academy for Jewish Research, Proceedings 1930-31* (New York: Kraus, 1968), 75-76.

88. Victor A. Tcherikover, ed., *Corpus Papyrorum Judaicarum*, 1 (Cambridge, Mass.: Harvard University Press, 1957): 8.

89. Schürer, 2:425 and n. 5.

90. Schürer, 2:425, n. 4.

In the Diaspora, the synagogue was called *proseuche,* the Greek word for prayer; as the term indicates, it was primarily a house of prayer, a place for religious worship. *Proseuche* was used almost exclusively by the Jews in Egypt from the 3rd century B.C.E. to the 1st century C.E. The term *synagoge,* "synagogue," to designate the place of assembly for public worship was first used in Palestine. By the mid-1st century C.E., it was also used in the Diaspora and soon became the accepted term.[91] Archaeological and inscriptional evidence attest that no single type of synagogue structure existed among the early synagogues either in the Diaspora or in Palestine. The size, architecture, and ornamentation of each synagogue depended to a great extent on the local customs and traditions of the regions in which they were built and the function and role that the synagogue served both within the Jewish and the social structures of the town or city of its location.[92] A universally accepted synagogue design does not occur until the 5th-6th centuries C.E. and in Palestine.[93] It is assumed that the earliest synagogues or *proseuchai* were simple structures lacking ornamentation. As the Jewish Diaspora began to gain wealth and social prestige, synagogues became more elaborate. There were small, modest, unadorned synagogues in the more rural areas and large, imposing, richly ornamented edifices in the large urban centers. The most majestic and wealthy were the great synagogues in Alexandria, in Sardis, in Antioch, Syria, and the Tiberias structure in Palestine. Evidence of synagogue ornamentation comes from archaeological discoveries from both Palestine and the Diaspora; it dates to the late 1st century B.C.E. and attests that the ornamentation similar to the architecture was influenced by local and regional traditions. Extensive pictorial art on wall murals, mosaics, and the plastic arts is exhibited in the synagogue ruins of the Hellenistic-Roman period both in Palestine and the Diaspora. Besides the representations of the sacred religious symbols such as the ark of the covenant, menorah, horns, and other symbols of religious ritual, there are figures and pagan motifs. The signs of the zodiac and the sun-god Helios, both of considerable importance in some pagan religions, were found in a number of ruins, as well as symbols of the vine, palm branches, peacocks, centaurs, and griffins. Hellenistic Judaism

91. Schürer, 2:440.

92. A. Thomas Kraabel, "Social Systems of Six Diaspora Synagogues," in *Ancient Synagogues: The State of Research,* ed. Joseph Gutmann. Brown Judaic Studies 22 (Chico: Scholars, 1981), 87-88.

93. Andrew R. Seager, "Ancient Synagogue Architecture: An Overview," in Gutmann, 42.

adopted the pagan symbols and gave them specific Jewish religious meanings. In the 2nd and 3rd centuries C.E., human images were used in biblical scenes. The human images were primarily, but not exclusively, biblical figures. Mythological figures also are depicted, the most popular of which was Orpheus, the Thracian harpist who tamed wild beasts with his music. He appears wearing a Phrygian cap and playing a harp, and symbolized salvation and eternal life.[94]

Information about the furnishings of the synagogue is scant and comes mainly from archaeological remains and pictoral representations. The most important furnishing in the synagogue was the ark, a portable chest in which the Torah scrolls and other sacred writings were kept. It was housed in an adjoining room and was brought into the synagogue as needed. In the synagogue, the ark was separated from the congregation by a veil or curtain that hung in front of it. Beginning in the 2nd-3rd centuries C.E., the ark became a permanent fixture and was set in a niche or apse in the synagogue wall that faced Jerusalem. The recess was set apart by a veil or curtain that hung in front of it or by a marble screen.[95] Next to the ark was the *bema*, a raised wooden platform on which stood the reader of the Torah. A wooden stand or lectern on the *bema* held the books of the Torah during the reading. Other permanent furnishings of the synagogue included the menorah, lamps, the horn that was blown on the first day of the New Year, and the trumpet used mostly on fast days. The congregation sat on stone or wooden benches that lined the walls of the synagogue or on floor mats. The number and organization of the benches differed among the diverse types of synagogue buildings. Seating during the service was according to one's age and rank, with the elders or distinguished members of the synagogue in the front and the others behind.[96] Most scholars assume that men and women sat separately, but no evidence exists, either archaeological or in the literature of Hellenistic Judaism, that any provision was made for such segregation.[97] In addition to the benches, many syna-

---

94. Schürer, 2:59, 443; and esp. Bezalel Narkiss, "Pagan Christian and Jewish Elements in the Art of Ancient Synagogues," in *The Synagogue in Late Antiquity*, ed. Lee I. Levine (Philadelphia: American Schools of Oriental Research, 1987), 183-88.

95. E. L. Sukenik, *Ancient Synagogues in Palestine and Greece* (1934, repr. Munich: Kraus, 1980), 52-57. See also S. Safrai and M. Stern, eds., *The Jewish People in the First Century*, 2 (Amsterdam: Van Gorcum, 1976): 938-39.

96. Safrai and Stern, 940; Sukenik, 58; Schürer, 2:446, 447 and n. 98.

97. Safrai and Stern, 939-40.

gogues had a special elevated seat of honor called the "seat of Moses," assumed to be reserved for the elder of the congregation.[98]

Synagogues were used for many purposes, the most important of which was for the reading, study, and interpretation of the Scriptures. Until the late 1st-early 2nd centuries C.E., both in Palestine and the Diaspora, services were held on the Sabbath morning, on feast days, and special occasions. Later, services also were held on Mondays and Thursdays.[99] Little is known about the service of the early synagogue. Most of the extant information concerning synagogue services comes from rabbinical sources and dates to the late 1st century C.E., when the service was expanded and given its established form.[100] The meager evidence indicates that the early service consisted of Israel's confession of faith, the *shema,* meaning "hear." It is so called from the opening words of the series of verses read from Deut. 6:4-9, "Hear O Israel: the Lord is our God, the Lord alone." After the *shema* came the "blessing," a series of 18 benedictions. The exact wording of the benedictions is unknown, since they, like the service, were not standardized until the late 1st century C.E.[101] During the recitation of the benedictions, the congregation stood and faced towards Jerusalem and the temple, a tradition that is presumed to date to the biblical period.[102] Private prayers were offered after the benedictions.[103] Evidence exists that an important part of the synagogue service in Alexandria was a reading from Scripture and its interpretation.[104] The practice of reading from the Prophets in addition to the Torah and the address or sermon that followed are affirmed for Palestinian synagogal services in the 1st century C.E.[105]

98. Schürer, 2: 441-42, n. 67. See also I. Renov, "The Seat of Moses," in *The Synagogue: Studies in Origins, Archaeology and Architecture,* comp. Joseph Gutmann (New York: Ktav, 1975), 233-38.

99. Safrai and Stern, 918-19; Arnaldo Momigliano, *On Pagans, Jews and Christians* (Middletown: Wesleyan University Press, 1987), 90.

100. For the development of the synagogal service, see Jakob J. Petuchowski, "The Liturgy of the Synagogue: History, Structure, and Contents," in *Approaches to Ancient Judaism,* ed. William Scott Green, 4: *Studies in Liturgy, Exegesis, and Talmudic Narrative.* Brown Judaic Studies 27 (Chico: Scholars, 1983): 1-64.

101. Samuel Sandmel, *Judaism and Christian Beginnings* (New York: Oxford University Press, 1978), 146-51; Petuchowski, 6-8; Safrai and Stern, 916.

102. Safrai and Stern, 938.

103. Petuchowski, 25.

104. Schürer, 2:448 and n. 102.

105. Schürer, 2:452-53; Momigliano, 90.

Greek was the standard language of the synagogue, both in the Diaspora and in Palestine, and the Scripture that was read was the Septuagint, the Greek translation. Hebrew was used in Palestine for the priestly blessing and for certain individual scriptural passages written for specific needs. It was not until the late 3rd-early 4th centuries that Hebrew began to replace Greek in the synagogue, and then not completely.[106]

The worship of the synagogue was the worship of the people. Unlike the worship in the Jerusalem temple that was dependent strictly on the priests, synagogal service was dependent on public participation. Any competent member of the congregation or even a visiting Jew was permitted to recite the *shema,* give the prayers, read and interpret the Scripture. Neither priest nor rabbi was required to conduct the service. Moreover, it substituted prayers for the sacrifices performed in the temple, and similar to other religions and cults of the Hellenistic-Roman period, the emphasis of the synagogue religion was concern more for individual salvation than for national prosperity. Through the personal salvation of the soul, it offered eternal life in the hereafter. The synagogue was Judaism's most significant adaptation, and it helped to transform Judaism from a typical state religion of antiquity to one of the most important and widespread of the Hellenistic-Roman world. During this period, the synagogue had become the center of the religious, cultural, social, and political life of the Jewish people. Nonetheless, the Jewish people, no matter in which country they resided, maintained a strong loyalty to the Jerusalem temple. This loyalty is reflected in the yearly half-shekel tax that was paid by every Jewish male 20 years and over to defray the expenses of the temple, and by the pilgrimages of the Jews from all parts of the world to Jerusalem, especially on the Holy Days. As the principal center of Jewish life, the synagogue was used, in addition to worship services, as a town meeting place where municipal business was conducted, matters of public interest were discussed, and legal concerns were adjudicated. It also served as a place for communal and festival meals. A number of synagogues had adjoining rooms that provided lodging for travelers.[107]

After the destruction of the temple and of Jerusalem, Judaism came

106. Tcherikover, *Corpus Papyrorum Judaicarum,* 1:101-2, 107-9 and n. 58; Davies and Finkelstein, 2:101-2.

107. Lee I. Levine, "The Second Temple Synagogue: The Formative Years," in *The Synagogue in Late Antiquity,* 14-15; Safrai and Stern, 942-43; Schürer, 2:447.

under the power and influence of the rabbis. The synagogue was further developed according to the rabbinic pattern and became one of the most important expressions of rabbinic Judaism. It was during this time, the restructuring of Judaism, that Hellenistic Judaism was cut off from mainstream Judaism. The rabbis rejected its apocalyptic views and wisdom theology, and by the middle of the 2nd century the production of such literature was greatly diminished. The Mishnah and the Tosefta were now the significant writings. Hellenistic Judaism ceased to exist after the Hellenistic-Roman period, but not before it was instrumental in the development and proliferation of another Hellenistic-Roman religion, Christianity.

Chapter IV

CHRISTIANITY

A. Primitive Christianity

Christianity arose after the resurrection of Jesus among a group of his followers who understood the event as an indication that Jesus was the long-awaited Messiah. Expectations of a messiah, the chosen or anointed of God from the house of David who would establish God's rule on earth, can be found in the writings of the Old Testament. During the Hellenistic-Roman period, and especially after the Roman conquest beginning in 63 B.C.E., this expectation intensified. It was most intense among the poor and pious Jews of Palestine, the socially and financially disadvantaged, who by the 1st century C.E. were in the majority.[1] To this group, anxious with expectation, Jesus brought his message of God's love, his acceptance of all, and the coming of a new world under God's rule, "the kingdom of God." Jesus' teaching, which was concentrated on rural Jewish people in the small towns and villages of Galilee, attracted many followers, some of whom considered him to be the Messiah. It also aroused the anger of both the Roman and Jewish authorities. The Romans accused Jesus of sedition for the claim that he was "King of the Jews," and the Jewish leaders accused him of blasphemy for claiming to be the Messiah. He was condemned to the death of the criminals and was nailed to a cross and left to die. A pious follower, Joseph of Arimathea, secured Jesus' body from the Roman au-

1. Robin Scroggs, "The Earliest Christian Communities as Sectarian Movement," in *Christianity, Judaism and other Greco-Roman Cults, 2: Early Christianity*, ed. Jacob Neusner. SJLA 12 (Leiden: E. J. Brill, 1975): 9ff.

thorities and buried it in a tomb. Later, when several of his faithful follow-ers visited the tomb, they found it empty.[2] This event convinced them that Jesus was truly the Messiah, the Anointed of God, who would redeem the Jewish people, destroy their oppressors, and establish God's rule, and they believed that this would happen soon. Thus, they were inspired to spread Jesus' message to their fellow Jews.

Rise of Christianity

The Christian movement began as an apocalyptic sect within Judaism. The Palestinian Jewish followers of Jesus, known as Nazarenes, a term derived from Jesus' hometown of Nazareth, were loyal Jews. They attended the temple services faithfully and observed the Mosaic laws, with one differ-ence: they understood the risen Jesus to be the Messiah. Their aim was to proclaim Jesus' message throughout Palestine. Christianity was spread be-yond Palestine to the Gentiles, the non-Jewish world, by the Jews of the Di-aspora who learned about Jesus during their pilgrimages to Jerusalem dur-ing the Jewish high holy days, and especially Passover, and carried the message of the risen Jesus to their homes throughout the Diaspora. Since the language of the Diaspora Jews was primarily Greek, they translated the Hebrew/Aramaic designations of Jesus into Greek. Palestinian Christianity referred to Jesus as Messiah, the one anointed by God, and *mar*, "Lord," an Aramaic honorific title used of a respected rabbi or individual with au-thority to judge.[3] The Hebrew term *mashiach*, "Messiah," became *Christos*, "Christ," the verbal adjective of the Greek verb *chrein*, "to anoint." Jesus was called Jesus the *Christos*. As Christianity developed, *Christos* was used as the proper name for Jesus and came to mean something more than Mes-siah, or eschatological judge and redeemer. The Aramaic *mar* was trans-lated *Kyrios*, a Greek term that had a greater significance than the Aramaic word, being used for gods, emperors, kings, and individuals of power and authority everywhere. The Hellenistic Jewish designation of Jesus as Christ the Lord gave him a divine aura, one of divine authority and power. More-

2. For a discussion of the empty tomb, see Hans von Campenhausen, "The Events of Easter and the Empty Tomb," in *Tradition and Life in the Church: Essays and Lectures in Church History* (Philadelphia: Fortress, 1968), 42-89.

3. See 1 Cor. 16:22, *Marana tha*, "Our Lord, come!," an Aramaic prayer dating from the earliest Palestinian Jewish Christians conveying the wish that the Messiah will come soon.

over, the Jewish Christians of the Diaspora called themselves *Christianoi*, "people of Christ," rather than Nazarenes. It was the Hellenistic Jewish Christian understanding of Jesus that the Diaspora Jewish Christians promulgated not only throughout the lands of the Jewish Diaspora but also the whole of the Gentile Hellenistic-Roman world. Principal among the Hellenistic Jewish Christian missionaries was the Apostle Paul.

Paul (ca. 10/11–ca. 64 C.E.) was a Hellenistic Jew from Tarsus, the capital of Cilicia in the southeastern corner of Asia Minor, a cosmopolitan, commercial, and university town with strong Greek and oriental influences. Paul knew both the Hellenistic-Roman and Jewish culture, but his formal education was Jewish. He was raised a Pharisee, trained in the law, and was a strong adherent to it. As a devout Pharisee, Paul considered blasphemous the claim that Jesus, a man condemned to the death of a criminal, was the Messiah, and he became a leading persecutor of the Christians. One day, while on a persecuting mission to Damascus, Paul had a vision of the resurrected Christ.[4] The experience convinced him that he had been called directly by the risen Christ and given the special task of spreading Christ's message to the Gentile world (Gal. 1:15-17). From that time on, Paul considered himself the apostle to the Gentiles and became, instead of a zealous persecutor of Christianity, its greatest defender. He traveled throughout the Hellenistic-Roman world, preaching and establishing communities bound together by Christ's message. The pace that he maintained was exhaustive, because he believed that the kingdom of God would be established soon and felt obligated to christianize as much of the inhabited world as was possible (Rom. 1:14-15).

Growth and Spread of Christianity

The early Jewish Christians understood Christianity in terms of its Jewish background and believed that a Christian must also be a Jew who obeyed the Mosaic law and observed the Jewish ceremonial rituals such as the dietary requirements and circumcision. Paul preached to the Gentiles in terms and concepts familiar to them and interpreted Christianity using terminology reminiscent of the contemporary mystery cults. Christ is the

---

4. Paul's experience is found in Acts 9:1-9; 22:3-11; 26:12-19, and alluded to in his letters, Gal. 1:15; 1 Cor. 15:8-9.

savior who came from heaven to earth to redeem mankind that was in bondage to an evil power. Salvation is achieved through fellowship with Christ that begins with the initiatory rite of baptism. Whoever accepts baptism shares in the death and resurrection of Christ. Through baptism, the individual dies to sin. He/she is free from all sin. All one's sins have been forgiven, and the individual is resurrected to a new life, a life in fellowship with the risen Lord who bestows on the individual the benefits and power that lead to eternal life (Rom. 6:2-11, 22-23). Thus, in Paul's understanding, the requirements of the Mosaic law were not necessary for salvation; salvation comes through faith in Christ (Gal. 3:23-26). Paul's attitude to the law and his strong insistence that Christians were free of the Mosaic law created a major problem between him and his Jewish Christian brethren, who persisted that Christians must keep some of the provisions of the law. Although a compromise was reached between Jewish and Paul's Christianity at the council of Jerusalem ca. 48,[5] the problem was not resolved until 70 and Rome's destruction of Jerusalem and the temple.

After that time, Jewish Christianity was diminished and marginalized. The majority of the Jewish Christians of Palestine migrated to Gentile lands. Many assimilated with the Gentile Christians. A small Jewish Christian community settled in Pella, a Greek settlement east of the Jordan River. They remained faithful to the Mosaic law and survived obscurely in the sect of the Ebionites, named after a Hebrew term meaning "the poor." The Christianity that existed after 70 spread and developed. It was a Hellenistic Gentile Christianity, a new and autonomous religion, free from any racial or national ties. It was a universal religion open to all of mankind, all races, all classes, the wealthy, poor, slave and free, both male and female, and based on the teachings of Paul. Less than 40 years after its beginning, Christianity, due largely to the missionary activities of Paul and his companions, had spread throughout the whole of the inhabited world. Although the earliest Christians, in general, concentrated their missionary activity toward their fellow Jews, it was among the Gentiles, the non-Jewish people, that the Christian mission had its greatest success.

Christianity developed within the framework of Hellenistic Judaism. It adopted Jewish monotheism, the concept of one supreme personal God; a rigorous moral code of conducting one's life derived from the ethical re-

---

5. There are two accounts of the council, one by Paul in Gal. 2:1-10 and one by the author of Acts 15:1-29.

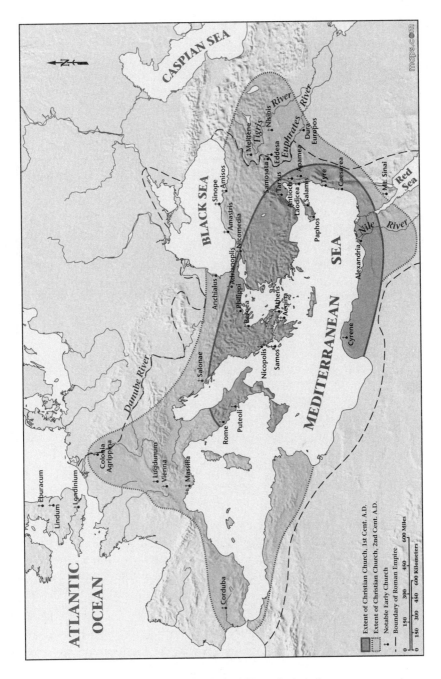

Map 4.1   Growth of the Early Church (2nd century C.E.)

quirements of the law; and the requirement of conversion, denouncing all other gods and taking a new life with a new meaning and new responsibilities. The Christian Bible was the Septuagint, the Greek translation of the Hebrew Scriptures. Early Christian communities were regarded as synagogues. The term *ekklesia*, "church," was first used by the author of the Gospel of Matthew, written ca. 85-90, to emphasize the Christian congregation called to salvation by God as an entity distinct from its Judaic origin.[6] Christian synagogue worship was similar to that of the Jews, but centered on the figure of Christ and Christ alone. Like the Jewish, the Christian synagogue was the gathering place of the community, a place of prayer, instruction, and inspiration. Synagogue worship included readings from the Septuagint, which was central, and prayers, many patterned after those of the Hellenistic Jews. Christians, like the Jews, prayed three times a day and fasted twice a week. The Christian fast days were Wednesday and Friday to commemorate Jesus' arrest and crucifixion, rather than Monday and Thursday as was the Jewish custom, especially of the Pharisees.[7] Sunday, the day of Christ's resurrection, became the holy day of the Christians instead of the Jewish Sabbath, which was Saturday.

Admission to and participation in the Christian community began with baptism, by which all sins were washed away and one was resurrected to a new life in Christ, a Christian. The baptized met regularly on Sundays, and sometimes on other days, to pray and worship together. After the Sunday worship they participated in a communal, fellowship meal referred to as the *agape*, or "feast of love," at which they partook of bread and wine. This meal served as a memorial of Christ's passion, a thanksgiving of his sacrifice, and a celebration of the Christians' fellowship with one another. The common meal bound the Christian community together and made them one body, the spiritual body of Christ.[8] Every member of the community who participated in the communal meal contributed to it in accordance with his/her means. From the end of the 1st century, the communal meal now known as the Eucharist took on a greater significance and was the center of Christian worship. It was regarded as the distinctively Christian sacrament and was understood as the very body and blood of Christ.

6. For the Judaic use of the term *ekklesia* vs. "synagogue," see Schürer, *The History of the Jewish People in the Age of Jesus Christ*, 2:429-30 n. 12.

7. Mark 2:18-20; Luke 18:11-12; Schürer, 2:483-84 and n. 109.

8. 1 Cor. 10:16-17.

The consecrated bread became his body and the wine his blood. By eating the bread and drinking the wine, a Christian joined his own flesh and blood with Christ's and attained an intimate union with him. Baptism and the Eucharist became the main sacraments of the Christian church. Beginning in the early 2nd century, when the church had formed into an ecclesiastical organization with a hierarchy, the sacraments were administered only by the church leaders. Christianity's acceptance of all people without distinction and its communal organization, a close-knit community bound together in fellowship and love, had a universal appeal during the Hellenistic-Roman period. Like the mystery cults, it satisfied the spiritual and emotional needs that were prevalent among the people during this time. By the end of the 2nd century, Christianity had spread throughout the major urban centers as well as the rural districts of the empire. As it expanded, the Christian way of life attracted the notice of both the Roman authorities and the general public.

B. Christianity's Encounter with Its Social World

Christians believed that they lived in a new creation, one inaugurated by Jesus and into which they entered at baptism. This new order was considered pure and sacred, and they, through baptism, had been sanctified and justified and were expected to live a life of moral purity, always striving for perfection. In contrast, the present world, the world outside that of the Christians, was considered evil and profane. Christians were opposed to many of its values and avoided it as much as possible. The Christians lived in exclusive, close-knit groups known as *ekklesiai*[9] and called one another "brothers" and "sisters." Although they continued to live in the cities and socially interacted with their non-Christian neighbors, the Christians lived their lives in accordance with the rules of the Christian community. They were expected to marry Christians and to remain monogamous, although existing marriages with pagan spouses were encouraged to be preserved. Some early Christians remained celibate in order to devote their lives to the spreading of the gospel, and others who did marry avoided cohabita-

---

9. The term *ekklesia* was used to designate both the individual Christian communities and the whole of the Christian movement. For a discussion of the *ekklesia*, see Wayne A. Meeks, *The First Urban Christians: The Social World of the Apostle Paul* (New Haven: Yale University Press, 1983), ch. 2.

tion. They considered it as typifying the continuation of the world that they were trying to escape. In their communities, Christians met together regularly to pray, and once a week to share a common meal in fellowship which in the course of time became the Eucharist. The Christians lived a life that was not typical of the general Hellenistic-Roman populace, but they were loyal subjects of the empire, law-abiding, somewhat inconspicuous, and did not openly display their beliefs and practices. As a result, until the last half of the 2nd century, little was known about them; they were generally considered a sect of Judaism and shared its privileges and unpopularity. Although the emperor Nero made the Christians scapegoats for the great fire of 64, until the end of the 2nd century persecutions were few and haphazard. The Roman authorities did not care very much what the Christians believed or did not believe, nor how they chose to live.

The Roman authorities, like the Greeks before them, were very tolerant and accepting of different religious views and beliefs and had absorbed many new and foreign cults. They respected a people's ancient customs and traditional way of life, and even made concessions to satisfy the requirement of Jewish monotheism. It was understood and accepted that Jews could not worship an emperor or foreign god because their national religion forbade it. The suppression of a cult or religion was not because of its religious beliefs, but for moral and/or political reasons such as the Bacchanalian conspiracy that was suppressed by the Roman senate in 186 B.C.E.[10] It did not matter what people believed or how they lived, as long as they stayed within the law. This meant acknowledging and paying homage to the state gods and to the emperor by participating in the state rites and ceremonies. Refusal to do so indicated disrespect for the empire and the divine powers that protected it and indifference for the welfare of the general public. The Romans[11] were very careful to honor their gods and believed that misfortunes were due to the gods' anger when they were dishonored or neglected. Like Judaism, Christianity's strict monotheism permitted worship only of its God. The Christians could not sacrifice to the state gods or emperor. However, although Rome accepted the Jewish monotheistic requirement because it was a national religion with an ancient tradition, Christianity could not make this claim. By the end of the 2nd century, it no longer had any national ties and did not have a tradition.

---

10. For a discussion of the Bacchanalia, see above the section on Dionysus in Chapter I B.
11. The term "Romans" is used to refer to the pagan citizens of the Roman Empire.

To the Roman authorities it was just another cult and, like them, subject to Roman law. The Christians' disrespect toward the protecting forces of the world in which they lived and its ancestral practices proclaimed them enemies of the state, and they were more aggressively persecuted.

Anti-Christian Polemics

During the reign of Marcus Aurelius (161-180), the empire began to experience several misfortunes. In 165, a plague swept throughout the empire decimating a large number of the population. Beginning in 167, barbaric forces were very much in evidence, and the emperor was forced to sell state property to pay for the wars. These calamities were blamed on the Christians' neglect of the gods and provoked major persecutions against them, the first in Asia Minor in 165 and another in Gaul in 177, and the rise of anti-Christian polemics. The oldest large-scale polemic was Celsus's *True Discourse,* written between 177 and 180, in which he expresses the common pagan views and concerns about the Christians.[12] A major portion of the work is preserved in fragments quoted in Origen's *Contra Celsum,*[13] a reply to Celsus written almost 80 years after Celsus's treatise. Celsus's purpose was to convince the Christians to return to the worship of the traditional gods. He hoped to accomplish this by skillfully discrediting the Christian faith item by item, proving it to be a religion of false doctrines and thus persuading the Christians back to paganism. Celsus feared that the religious and political isolation of the Christians was creating a division among the populace, weakening the empire, and causing danger to the welfare and security of the state (*Cels.* 8.69-75). Only through a united effort and a united people could the dangers threatening the empire be averted. Celsus knew his subject well. An analysis of his quotations reveals that he had some familiarity with the Old Testament, knew the four Gospels, especially that of Matthew, and the Christian literature of the period (4.52; 8.15).

Celsus begins by accusing Christianity of being a secret society and

---

12. A comprehensive study of how the pagans viewed Christianity is found in Robert L. Wilken, *The Christians as the Romans Saw Them* (New Haven: Yale University Press, 1984). For Celsus's polemic, see also Antonía Tripolitis, *Origen: A Critical Reading* (New York: Peter Lang, 1985), ch. 4.

13. The text used is Origen, *Contra Celsum,* trans. Henry Chadwick (1965; repr. Cambridge: Cambridge University Press, 1980).

thus illegal (*Cels.* 1.1). The members wall themselves off from the rest of mankind, are bound together by some mysterious intimacy, and recognize each other by private signs (8.2; 1.1ff.). Celsus then proceeds to discredit the character and teaching of Jesus and the historical account of the gospel. Christians, he claims, believe and accept doctrines without examination. Blindly they accept the claims of Jesus that he is the Son of God, a belief that is not based on logic and reasoning and is worthy of its adherents, individuals who are in the main uneducated (1.26-27). Concerning Jesus and the claims about him, Celsus asserts that most were fabricated by Jesus, and there are no credible witnesses nor reliable sources to establish the truth of the events of his life that the Christians believe proclaim him divine. Jesus' so-called divine powers with which he performed miracles were developed in Egypt where, because of his extreme poverty, he migrated and hired himself out as a workman (1.28). His miracles are not any different or better than those accomplished by the Egyptian trained sorcerers (1.67-68). Even Jesus' resurrection is not a unique event. Celsus gives numerous examples of other figures in the ancient world that also have been credited with similar feats. Moreover, the event had been witnessed by a hysterical woman (2.55; 3.31-32). The Christian accounts of Jesus' life and ministry are neither reliable nor unique. They are similar to the other countless legends told about men and heroes, and like them were devised by his followers to glorify him and his deeds (3.22, 31-32). In fact, contends Celsus, Christianity does not offer anything new. What the Christians claim as unique has been done or said before. Their doctrines are misunderstandings and corruptions of the ancient traditions (3.16; 5.65). Even the Christians' ethics, of which Celsus approved, contain nothing that is impressive or new. They are common to all philosophers and better expressed by them (1.4; 7.58).

The Christian concept to which Celsus most strongly objected was the doctrine of the incarnation. According to him, this was an absurd and disgraceful notion. If, as tradition claims, God is good, beautiful, and blessed and possesses these qualities in perfection, a descent to the material world implies a change, one from good to bad, from beautiful to shameful, from happiness to misfortune, and from what is best to what is most wicked. Since God is immortal and immutable, he is not subject to alteration. Thus, he is not able to undergo this change (4.14).[14] Moreover, what pur-

---

14. Celsus's understanding of God is the popular concept of God held both by pagan philosophers and Christians of the time.

pose would the descent of God serve? God is knowledgeable of all that happens on earth and can remedy what is wrong by divine power. There is no need to come down to earth to reform mankind (4.3). Furthermore, why would God after numerous years of inactivity decide to judge humanity? Did he not care before (4.8)? Why, if God wanted to save mankind from evil, did he not send his spirit throughout the world, rather than to one group only, and of all people, the Jews (6.78, 80)? Celsus dismissed the idea of the incarnation as untenable and blasphemous and the Christian view of God as ludicrous and impious (6.78; 7.14; 8.14-15).

After attacking Christianity's beliefs, Celsus ends his treatise by imploring the Christians not to forget loyalty and support to the emperor and the Roman state. He appeals to the Christians not to create difficulties for the emperor by refusing to serve in the army or to accept public office, but to help and cooperate with him to maintain justice and to preserve the laws and religion (8.73, 75). The Christians' lack of cooperation and their "atheism," their refusal to worship the state's gods and to give divine honor to the emperor, were perceived by the rulers and masses of the empire as a deliberate expression of political subversion. Celsus feared that the Christians' attitude and continued growth would create a new social order, a state within the state, with its own laws and patterns of behavior. This would disrupt the bonds of society and be disastrous to the empire, especially at a time when it was in grave danger from the barbarians. Celsus asks the Christians not to disregard Homer, who long ago proclaimed, "Let there be one ruler, one king,"[15] implying the emperor. If everyone acted as the Christians, nothing would prevent the emperor from being abandoned and left solitary and desolate. Then the affairs of the world would fall into the hands of the most lawless and savage barbarians (3.55; 8.63-75). Celsus's main concern about Christianity was its profound social and political consequences, consequences which he considered most disastrous to the Roman Empire.

Early Christian Apologies

Despite the pagan prejudices against Christianity, forcefully expressed in Celsus's extant quotations, the Christian movement continued to expand and to attract individuals from all walks of life. As early as the mid-2nd

15. *Iliad* 2.205.

century, it included among its ranks a number of philosophically trained minds. These individuals set out to define and explain Christianity and its beliefs in terms comprehensible to the educated pagan populace. In the process, they began to express the Christian doctrines within the contemporary philosophical views, in particular the Middle Platonic.[16] Through their writings, known as *apologiai* or "apologies," they hoped to vindicate Christianity from the pagan slanders, criticisms, and the intermittent persecutions of the Christians, as well as to provide Christianity with a historical past. One of the main pagan objections to Christianity was that it was a modern innovation without a history or tradition and thus illegal. The Apologists attempted to show that Christianity is not something new, but the restatement and confirmation of truths that humanity had always held or sought. It is not a new religion, but the true religion, the true philosophy. In his *Dialogue with Trypho* written ca. 160, Justin (ca. 100/110–ca. 165), the most important and most voluminous of the early apologists, explains his conversion to Christianity as a conversion to the "true philosophy." Disillusioned with the various philosophical schools of the time in which he had studied — Stoic, Peripatetic, Pythagorean, and Platonic — he became a Christian, and found in Christianity the philosophical truth for which he was searching (*Dial.* 8).[17] In addition to vindicating Christianity, the apologies are invitations to the true philosophy, and are directed to all who are interested to find it and to make it their way of life. Most of the apologies were addressed to the emperor or other pagan notables, but there is no evidence that they were read by any except Christians, individuals contemplating becoming Christians, and critics of Christianity such as Celsus who used them as material to refute Christianity. Some scholars claim that Celsus's anti-Christian polemic was written in response to Justin's defense of Christianity.[18]

16. See above, Chapter I C.

17. The early Greek apologists whose works have survived are Aristides (fl. ca. 145), Justin (ca. 100-165), Tatian (ca. 110-172), Athenagoras (fl. ca. 170-180), and Theophilus of Antioch (ca. 115–ca. 190). The Greek text is from Daniel Ruiz Bueno, ed., *Padres Apologistas Griegos* (Madrid: Editorial Catolica, 1954). An English translation of their works can be found in Alexander Roberts and James Donaldson, eds., *Ante-Nicene Fathers* 1-2, 8 (Grand Rapids: Wm. B. Eerdmans, 1979). In addition, fragments from the works of Quadratus (fl. ca. 125), Melito of Sardis (fl. ca. 160–ca. 190), and Appolinaris of Hierapolis (fl. ca. 170-180) are preserved in Eusebius's *Hist. eccl.*.

18. Carl Andresen, *Logos und Nomos: Die Polemik des Kelsos wider das Christentum* (Berlin: Walter de Gruyter, 1955), 308-92.

A number of apologies were written between 130 and 200. Some are extant in their entirety and others only in a few fragments or quotations. The works differ in their treatment and emphases, but all share a common denominator: to demonstrate that Christianity is a philosophy, a way of life in conformity with reason and truth, and that its emphasis is the right conduct of the individual within the community and the state. It is the true philosophy, older and superior to all other philosophies, traditional religions, and beliefs, proof of which is found in the wisdom of all the ancient traditions. Their arguments, best expressed in the works of Justin, begin with the universal Logos or divine Reason that existed with God from the primordial beginning. In contemporary philosophical terms, the apologists describe God as transcendent, beyond all being, unchanging, unbegotten, perfect, and eternal. Thus, he could not possibly come into contact with the world of change and dissolution,[19] but only through the Logos, the divine wisdom through whom God created and ordained the universe, and which serves as the mediator between God and the cosmos.[20] A seed of the Logos is implanted in every individual. It is this "germinal logos" or reason that unites an individual to God and gives him/her the ability to apprehend the truth. All who lived in conformity with reason were, in a sense, Christians before Christ, including the prophets of the Old Testament and the Greek poets and philosophers.[21] In particular the prophets, who preceded the writers of ancient Greece, in their inspired writings taught the same truths that were subsequently taught by Christ. The poets and philosophers borrowed their wisdom from Moses and the prophets, but sometimes seem to have misunderstood the prophetic writings. This is evident from the fact that they contradict themselves. Thus the Greek writers were able to arrive at fragmentary facets of the truth.[22]

The Logos then became incarnate in its entirety in Jesus Christ, who revealed the ultimate truth and fulfilled and corrected all the truths that were partially apprehended by the ancient poets and philosophers. The principal evidence for this is found in the Old Testament prophecies. By his virgin birth and in his earthly career, Christ fulfilled in detail the predictions made by the prophets hundreds and even thousands of years be-

19. *Dial.* 4.1; 60.5; 127.
20. *2 Apol.* 6.3.
21. *1 Apol.* 46.
22. *1 Apol.* 44.59-60.

fore, and conclusively proved the truth of their teachings as well as his own.[23] As the incarnate divine Reason, Christ's teachings are superior to all human teachings, and they are universal and as old as creation.[24] According to Justin, there has always been only one truth, given to mankind in the very beginning, but often apprehended in a fragmentary and abstract form. This truth is now fully realized in Christianity, the true philosophy.[25] Justin requests of the emperors to live up to their reputation as pious men and philosophers and to treat the Christians, the followers of the true philosophy, as they would all others who live in accordance with reason and truth.[26] Similarly, the apologist Melito of Sardis, in his *Apology* to the emperor Marcus Aurelius written in the 170s, considered Christianity an auspicious blessing to the empire and asserted that if the empire was to continue in its splendid and glorious manner, the emperor must protect the Christian philosophy and respect it along with all the other religions just as his predecessors did, with the exception of Nero and Domitian.[27] The aim of the apologists was to vindicate Christianity and to ask that it be judged by the same standards as other religious philosophies. In spite of the apologists' efforts, criticism of Christianity and persecution of the Christians continued and was accelerated during the 3rd century.

C. The Development of Christianity into a Systematic Religious Philosophy

Throughout the 3rd century, beginning in the reign of Septimus Severus (193-211), the empire witnessed a series of appalling military, social, and economic conditions: barbarian invasions, bloody civil wars, various recurring plagues, famines, and economic crises. These calamities were blamed on the Christians who, it was believed, had offended the gods by ignoring them and not paying homage to them. The result was a systematic, empire-wide governmental persecution of the Christians. It began in 249 during the reign of Decius (249-251) and continued until the great persecution under Diocletian (284-305) and Galerius (203-311). During this

23. *1 Apol.* 30; 31; 53.
24. *2 Apol.* 10.1; *Dial.* 43.1ff.
25. *2 Apol.* 13.
26. *1 Apol.* 2; 68.
27. *Hist. eccl.* 4.26.7-8.

time, the polemics against the Christians increased in hostility. Principal among them was the bitter work *Against the Christians* written by the Neo-Platonist Porphyry ca. 270. This work was imitated by many and dominated the philosophical debates between pagans and Christians for almost a century. Yet, despite the formidable prejudice against Christianity, the movement continued to grow steadily and to develop. During this period, Christianity established an organized ecclesiastical hierarchy, it was in the process of standardizing a scriptural canon, and church edifices began to be built, replacing the private homes as places of worship. Christianity had become what Celsus had feared, a state within the state. As it organized and established itself within the empire, Christianity realized that it had to come to terms with the social world in which it existed. It had to present a reasoned case as an acceptable philosophy, a way of life, comparable to the contemporary philosophical schools that by the 2nd century had developed into a religion based on reason. Their aim was to prepare individuals to live in a hostile world, and emphasized ethics and moral discipline rather than metaphysics or epistemological concerns.[28] The 2nd-century apologists took the first step in this direction. They employed philosophical arguments in their defense of Christianity, but they did not produce a systematic theology. This challenge was undertaken by the Christian Platonist of the Alexandrian school, Origen.

Synthesis of Biblical Christianity and Platonism

Little is known of Christian activities in Alexandria until ca. 180. By that time, according to Eusebius,[29] a school for catechumens existed in the city under the leadership of Pantaenus, a converted Stoic philosopher. No further information is known about Pantaenus or of the origins of the school. Initially, the school consisted of a voluntary, unofficial group of scholars interested in the study and exposition of the Scriptures. Its aim was to prepare the catechumens for service to the church. Sometime shortly before 200, Pantaenus gave the leadership of the school to his pupil Clement and left Alexandria. Clement (ca. 150–ca. 215) was also a convert to Christianity who after his conversion traveled throughout the Roman world studying

28. The religious philosophies of the time are discussed above in Chapter I C.
29. *Hist. eccl.* 5.10.1-4.

with a number of different Christian teachers. The last was Pantaenus, whom he considered the greatest of them all, and so Clement remained in Alexandria.[30] Under Clement's leadership and then that of Origen who succeeded him, the school developed into a center of Christian scholarship, a center of sacred science comparable in academic quality to the best pagan philosophical schools. Clement was a strong advocate of philosophy and considered it consistent with Christianity, which he regarded as the end to which all contemporary philosophy had been progressing. Similar to the apologists, Clement used philosophical terms to interpret Christianity, but he was not a systematic thinker. His writings, especially the *Stromateis* or "Miscellanies," in which he mostly discusses theological questions, consists of unsystematic notes that he collected from the various Christian teachers with whom he had studied before settling in Alexandria. At the end of his work the *Paedagogus* or "Tutor," Clement mentions his intention to produce a work that would contain a systematic exposition of Christian doctrine.[31] This intention was never realized, and the task was left to his successor, Origen.

Origen (ca. 185–ca. 254)[32] was born in Egypt, probably in Alexandria, of parents who were converts to Christianity. The principal source of his early life is found in the sixth book of Eusebius's *Ecclesiastical History.* Eusebius claims to have derived the biographical information from official documents, letters of Origen which he had collected, and information received from individuals who were acquainted with Origen.[33] According to this account, Origen, whose nickname was Adamantios, "Man of Steel," was raised as a Christian and was educated in the Scriptures as well as in all the branches of secular learning. In fact, it is claimed that he attended the lectures of Ammonius Saccas, who laid the foundation for the Neo-Platonic school.[34] When Origen was not quite 17, his father Leonides was martyred during the persecution of Septimus Severus in 202. His father's property was confiscated by the state, and Origen, his mother, and six younger brothers were left in poverty with Origen as the sole support.[35] The follow-

---

30. *Hist. eccl.* 5.11.

31. *Paed.* 3.12.97.

32. A large portion of the section on Origen is summarized from my text, *Origen: A Critical Reading.*

33. *Hist. eccl.* 6.2.1; 33; 3.3.

34. *Hist. eccl.* 6.19.2.

35. *Hist. eccl.* 6.2.15.

ing year, 203, Demetrius, bishop of Alexandria, designated Origen the head of the catechetical school, which was now under the bishop's jurisdiction. Origen remained in the post for several years and attracted numerous students from all philosophical schools and religions by his erudite teaching and the stern ascetic simplicity of his mode of life.[36]

In addition to his administrative and teaching duties, first in Alexandria and later in Caesarea, where he founded another catechetical school, Origen produced a voluminous body of writings of a diverse and complex nature. His works include exegetical and critical works on the text of the Old and New Testaments, homilies, commentaries, apologies in defense of Christianity, and works on Christian dogma or religious philosophy. Origen was the first Christian systematic commentator and interpreter of the Bible. His homilies and commentaries covered almost the entire Greek Scriptures, both of the Old and New Testaments. One of his most important scriptural works is the *Hexapla*, a sixfold edition of the Old Testament in both Greek and Hebrew that is considered to be the first attempt in the field of biblical criticism. Origen is also credited for the first coherent systematic presentation of Christianity. Most of his works, however, have been lost or destroyed, and many of those that survive are preserved in 4th-century Latin translations, several of which are inaccurate. Of the Greek fragments that have survived, the authenticity of several has been questioned and others have proven to be summaries of the original material. The only work that exists in its entirety and in Greek is his apologetic work against Celsus, *Contra Celsum.*

Origen was first and foremost a biblical scholar. He considered the Scriptures divine, a reflection of the invisible or divine world and the only means by which an individual could attain the divine truths. As a result, the prime purpose of Scripture is not to present a literal meaning or a narrative of historical events, but to convey divine and eternal truths that are hidden under the letter of Scripture.[37] It was of utmost importance to Origen to reveal and correctly expound and interpret the hidden meaning of the Scriptures, and he considered it his primary task, which he accomplished by means of allegorical interpretation. Allegorical exegesis had

36. *Hist. eccl.* 6.3.7.

37. *Princ.* 4.3.4ff. Origen's works are from the edition of Paul Koetschau, *Origenes Werkes.* Die Griechischen Christlichen Schriftseller der Ersten Drei Jahrhunderte 2/1-12 (Leipzig: J. C. Hinrichs, 1891-1955); and C. H. E. Lommatzsch, *Origen Opera Omnia* (Berlin: Sumtibus Haude et Spener, 1831-1848), 25 vols.

been practiced and encouraged by Clement, who regarded it as part of the church's rule of faith, and attributed both a literal and a spiritual meaning to the Scriptures.[38] Origen continued the Alexandrian tradition of allegorizing the Scriptures, and found their true and deeper meaning in the philosophical concepts which lie beneath the literal and historical husk. In this manner, he attempted to bring into accord, systematically, the philosophy of Christianity with its documents.

According to Origen, Scripture has both an obvious, literal meaning and a hidden or allegorical one. The allegorical meaning is further divided into the moral and spiritual. Thus Scripture generally has three meanings or senses, the literal, the moral, and the spiritual. All of Scripture contains a spiritual or deeper meaning, but every scriptural passage does not have a literal meaning. The reason for this is that the literal meaning often proves to be an impossibility. Origen adhered to the general rule that whenever a scriptural passage entails something impossible, absurd, or unworthy of God, the literal meaning should be disregarded and the passage should be interpreted allegorically.[39] Moreover, when there is both a spiritual and literal or historical meaning, the spiritual is of greater importance than the narrative of historical events.[40] In some instances, however, the obvious or literal meaning is the conclusive one. This is true when the text refers to a historical or actual event. Thus in reading the Scriptures, an individual must discern whether a passage is to be understood literally or allegorically by carefully investigating to what extent the literal meaning is true and possible. An individual's ability to perceive the hidden meaning of Scripture is dependent on one's spiritual development.[41]

Origen's textual and critical studies of the Old and New Testaments, the *Hexapla,* and commentaries in which he attempted to give the three meanings of each scriptural verse — literal, moral, and spiritual — helped to establish the scientific study and interpretation of the Scriptures. His use of allegory to determine the spiritual sense of Scripture did much to preserve the Scriptures for the church, and to establish an understanding of the relationship between the Old and New Testaments. Much of the Old Testament in its purely literal interpretation was difficult, if not impossi-

38. *Strom.* 5.8ff.; 14.
39. *Princ.* 4.3.5.
40. *Princ.* 4.3.5.
41. *Princ.* pref. 8. For a more detailed explanation of the threefold meaning of the Scriptures, see Tripolitis, *Origen,* ch. 3.

ble, to vindicate as Christian literature, and the literal exegeses of either Testament could not be defended against the criticism of the educated pagans. Although Origen was not the first Christian theologian to employ allegory in the explication of the Scriptures, he was the first to formulate it into a system. The scientific method of allegorical interpretation that he established influenced the interpretation of Scripture both in the East and in the West. Moreover, the use of allegory made it possible for Origen to show the compatibility of the philosophical culture of the time with the gospel, within the confines of the Christian tradition.

In the area of religious philosophy, Origen was the first to attempt to present a logical system of the Christian pronouncements of God, the world, and mankind, and to attempt to harmonize theology, cosmology, and anthropology. The principal works in this attempt are *De principiis* or "First Principles," in which he undertakes to provide a coherent broad interpretation of Christian doctrine in defense of orthodox Christianity against the gnostic heresies; and *Contra Celsum*, in which he explains the difference between Celsus's Platonism and his Platonic Christianity. Origen's thought is not a complete system of formulated doctrines and dogmas as found in later theological works, but it is the first attempt to synthesize Christianity and Platonism. Many of his views are exploratory rather than dogmatic. They are possible answers to various Christian beliefs that were not answered by dogma or tradition. In his search for possible answers, Origen relied heavily on Greek philosophy. He adopted the popular Greek philosophical ideas of his time that could serve as possible tools to explain the Christian faith. These ideas he reshaped, revised, and modified in accordance with his understanding of the Christian beliefs.

Origen's thought begins with the idea of the supreme reality, God, and ends with the concept of the individual soul's union with him. Following the Platonic tradition of his time, Origen stresses the absolute immateriality of God. God alone is unbegotten, a simple and indivisible intellectual nature, permitting no addition of any kind. He is absolute unity, the source from which all intellectual nature or mind commences.[42] God is incorporeal, eternal, immutable, and impassible, beyond space and time.[43] He transcends all, self-sufficient and self-contained, beyond thought and being, greater than anything mankind can understand or that can be mea-

42. *Princ.* 1.1.6; *Comm. Jo.* 1.20ff.; *Cels.* 4.14.
43. *Cels.* 6.62, 64; 7.38ff.

sured. Although transcendent and incomprehensible, God can be known through the Son or Logos and through the beauty of his works. His providence is felt by all, and he manifests himself through the Son to those whom he considers worthy, in accordance with their ability to perceive him.[44] Since he is absolutely transcendent, and a complete unity and simplicity, God could not directly create or have contact with a multiple and complex universe. An intermediary is needed who is midway between God, the uncreated, primal unity, and the created world of the many. This intermediary is the Son or Logos, who possesses both aspects at once, the unity of God and the multiplicity of the world.[45]

The Son or Logos is the firstborn of God, the perfect image and wisdom of the Father, the sum total of his world ideas. As such, the Logos has existed with God from the beginning as his wisdom, and has no beginning in time. There was never a time when the Logos did not exist. He is eternally generated from the essence of the Father without diminishing the Father's essence. As the image of God's power, the Logos is the same in essence as the Father or *homoousios,* but he is less than the Father. He is everything that the Father is, but on a different or lower level, and is often described as a "second God."[46] Similar to other contemporary Greek philosophers, Origen assumes the fundamental principle that the product is always inferior to the producer. Thus, the Logos is for Origen a hypostasis of the Father. He exists substantially and essentially according to his own substantial reality, numerically distinct from the Father, the second in number.[47] The first creation of God through the Logos is the Holy Spirit, which proceeds from the Logos and is related to him as the Logos is related to the Father, i.e., inferior to him. Proceeding from the Logos, the Holy Spirit is eternal and incorporeal, and is equal in honor and dignity to God and the Logos.[48] God, the Logos, and the Holy Spirit form an eternal, divine triad. They are three distinct beings possessing a unity of essence, will, and thought.[49]

The divine Logos became incarnated in Jesus and assumed a mortal body and a human soul. This resulted in the inseparable union of the soul

44. *Princ.* 1.1.5-9; *Cels.* 7.42.
45. *Cels.* 3.34.
46. *Princ.* 1.2.2-13; *Cels.* 5.39; 6.64.
47. *Cel.* 8.12.
48. *Princ.* pref. 4; 1.3.5.
49. *Cels.* 8.12.

of Jesus with the Logos, which Origen compares to that of a mass of iron which has been placed in the fire and ceaselessly flows with a white-hot heat.[50] The union of the divine and human nature formed a single personality, Christ, the God-man, a composite being, at once both totally human and totally divine.[51] Origen understood the purpose of the incarnation as the deification of humanity, the union of all individuals with the divine Logos, representing God's preeminent act of redemption of mankind. It was the Logos' greatest attempt to reconcile mankind with God by becoming the example and model for its salvation, the means by which mankind can return to their spiritual state.[52] The various functions and attributes of the incarnated Logos are as a ladder by which the individual soul advances step by step from its present bodily state to pure spirit, achieved through the soul's diligent imitation of Christ and Christ's continual help and guidance.

Origen's doctrine of the soul, its nature, and destiny is his most original synthesis of Platonism and the Bible and his most controverted. He taught that all souls were created from all eternity as pure spirits, perfect, equal, and free, and participants in the life of the Logos and in perfect communion with God. However, through the exercise of their free will they fell away from God, and this caused them to lose their initial unity and equality and to take on various types of forms and material textures. The material and form of a soul's body were determined by the degree of its estrangement from the Divine.[53] Thus, the diversity existing within the created order, the various conditions existing among individuals, is a result of the differences among the souls in the degree of their fall. An individual's status of birth and the situations that befall him during his lifetime should not be directly attributed to God or to chance, but to the soul's conduct in its preexistent state.[54]

Simultaneously with the bodies of the fallen beings, God created the material universe to serve as a place for educating and disciplining the souls, a place through which and from which the souls must rise to apprehend and become once again a part of the world of truth and ultimate re-

50. *Cels.* 2.9; *Princ.* 2.6.6.

51. *Princ.* 2.6.3; *Cels.* 1.66.

52. *Princ.* 4.4.4; *Cels.* 6.68.

53. *Princ.* 2.9.1-6; 4.4.9; *Cels.* 1.32. For a detailed account of the soul's fall and return, see Antonia Tripolitis, *The Doctrine of the Soul,* pt. 3.

54. *Princ.* 1.8.1; 2.2.1;, 9.2-3.

ality.[55] However, this created order is temporary, an intermediate or passing phase. All souls will one day be purified and reunited with their Creator. At this time, the visible material universe will cease to exist. The creation of another world order is dependent on the freedom of the will of the rational beings. Having fallen from God before, it is possible that they might fall again. If so, a new world order will be needed in order for providence to again redeem the fallen beings and bring them back to the Creator.[56] Thus, the creation of the world becomes a constant, unceasing act, the endless succession of world orders, one following the other.

The doctrine of the *apokatastasis,* as Origen calls the restoration of all rational beings to their original state of purity and equality, is unique to his thought and is most typical of his philosophical/theological speculation. It is determined by the principle that the end should resemble the beginning. Accordingly, since all rational souls come from the divine world, so all souls, at an appointed time known only to God, will be completely purified and will voluntarily return to their original state of perfection.[57] No rational soul is excluded from this perfect unity in God, no matter how much it might have fallen into sin. Created in the image of God, all rational souls share or partake of the divine essence. Even though it has been estranged from God, each rational being always retains within it a spark of the divine, a germ of goodness, by which it maintains a certain kinship or affinity to God and which in its essence is inaccessible to evil.[58] At the universal restoration, the purified souls will no longer be conscious of anything other than God, who will be the mode and measure of their every movement. God's rule will be universal, and he will be all in all.[59]

Origen maintains that the individual's goal in life should be to realize his true divine nature and to strive to regain his original pure state and likeness to God. This is a long and arduous task, for the soul is continually beset by temptations that try to lure it into sin. In order for the goal to be achieved, mankind's steady and persistent effort is required, together with God's continuous guidance and help. Origen views the soul's ascent as a gradual inner, spiritual development, a process by which the soul diligently

---

55. *Princ.* 3.5.4-5; *Cels.* 7.50.
56. *Princ.* 1.3.18; *Comm. Jo.* 10.42.
57. *Princ.* 1.6.1; 2.10.8.
58. *Princ.* 4.4.9-10; *Comm. Jo.* 32.11.
59. *Princ.* 2.11.7; 3.6.2-3.

strives to purify itself, a continual advancement towards the good. First, it purifies itself morally, then with the grace of God it develops the sense or knowledge to discern the real from the temporal. As it continues to be illuminated by the Logos, it advances forward until it comes to live purely in the spirit and unites with the Logos. Origen emphasizes that, every step of the way, the soul requires the grace of God. Alone, the soul does not possess a sufficiently strong will or the ability to obtain union with God through its own insight, self-knowledge, or by merely imitating Christ.[60] The soul's ascent to its Creator is not confined to this life; it continues after death. There is no soul that has been completely purified in this life.[61] Final union with God can be achieved only after death. The way by which the soul ascends progressively to God, whether in its earthly life or in its journey from this life to the life beyond, Origen finds in the Scriptures, set forth in mystical or symbolic terms.[62] In Origen, the synthesis of philosophy and Christianity was complete.

Christian Platonism and Its Opponents

Origen was harshly criticized by both the pagan intellectuals and by the Christians. One of his worst pagan critics was the Neo-Platonist Porphyry (ca. 232-305), whom he had met when Porphyry was a very young man and whose work he knew. Porphyry could not forgive Origen for abandoning Hellenism, which alone was lawful, to become a proponent of that barbarous enterprise, Christianity. He accuses Origen not only of apostatizing from the ancient tradition, but also of using Greek philosophy to rationalize and defend Christianity, which Porphyry considered a crude, barbaric superstition.[63] Porphyry's 15-volume anti-Christian work, *Against the Christians*, was in response to Origen's vindication of Christianity, espe-

60. *Cels.* 7.33, 42-44; *Princ.* 3.2.2, 5.
61. *Princ.* 2.11.6-7; 3.6.6; *Hom. Num.* 25.6.
62. The soul's spiritual journey is described in detail in Origen's homilies on Exodus, Numbers, and homilies and commentary on the Song of Songs. In particular, the 27th homily on Numbers presents a detailed explanation of the 42 stages of the soul's ascent from the earthly to the spiritual life. This is accomplished through the allegorical interpretation of Israel's exodus from Egypt to the Promised Land.
63. Porphyry's allegations are from his *Against the Christians,* now lost. Fragments of his work are quoted by Eusebius in *Hist. eccl.* 6.19.5-8.

cially in *Contra Celsum*.[64] Among Porphyry's major criticisms was the habit of the Christians to platonize Christianity and to use allegory to interpret the Hebrew Scriptures. This practice he attributes to Origen, who is his main target in the polemic.[65] Porphyry criticizes Origen for unscrupulously reading all the Greek mysteries into the Hebrew writings and giving a Greek meaning to all the foreign tales.[66]

Christianity's harshest criticism of Origen concerned his doctrine of the world and of the individual soul. Origen's view of the world's eternality, without beginning or end, and the succession of world orders was considered too speculative and philosophical, and he was accused of being unduly influenced by Greek philosophy. In particular, his doctrine of the preexistence of the soul and its fall into matter was rejected as heretical. It was greatly controverted by the church and finally resulted in Origen's unjust condemnation by the Fifth Ecumenical Council of 553. Origen wrote at a time when Christianity was in one of the most difficult times in its history, when it was in the throes of defining its doctrines against the pagan polemics. Yet although the dialogue between paganism and Christianity was often harsh and vigorous, Christianity profited from it. It introduced a dialectic element into Christian thinking that helped the Christians to understand the tradition they were defending, to systematize their fundamental beliefs, and to formulate a distinctive Christian teaching. Origen was a pioneer in this attempt. He was the first to present a Christian philosophy/theology, a coherent, logical system of the Christian account of God, the world, and mankind, and frequently employed the contemporary philosophical concepts to express his Christian thought within the context of a Hellenistic-Roman rationality. Although during this time many views were discussed concerning God, the world, and mankind, the church had not yet given formal expression to these matters. It was Origen's intent to present possible answers, principles, and predominating ideas and tendencies, but not to establish definite doctrinal views.[67] He was often too daring and too speculative, but no matter how bold his views were, they were meant as suggestions rather than positive statements. Many of the views for which he was criticized were put forward for

64. *Hist. eccl.* 4.1-4.
65. *Hist. eccl.* 4.1-4.
66. *Hist. eccl.* 19.5-8.
67. Origen's intent is stated in *Princ.* pref. 3.

discussion and investigation, not as established dogma. Moreover, the theses that were condemned by the Council of 553 were not his own but the development and interpretation of his views in the 4th century by the monk Evagrius Ponticus (345-399).

Despite the many controversies surrounding Origen, he is considered one of the greatest theologians of the church, and no one, neither advocate nor adversary, could escape his influence. His contributions are many and include all areas of Christian thought. He, more than anyone of his time, was influential in establishing and defining the church's doctrines and the thought of the early church. Although rejected by the Council of 553, Origen's doctrines of the soul, its nature, and various levels of participation in the divine life served as a foundation for the teachings of the later Fathers on the nature of grace. He was also influential in the development of the theology of the spiritual life. He is considered the founder of that theology and the forerunner of monasticism. Origen was the first to describe in careful detail each step of the individual soul's spiritual journey on its return to the Divine. His ascetic concepts and mystical views of the soul influenced the thought of many Christian thinkers, both Eastern and Western, who succeeded him, and had a great and lasting influence on the development of the monastic life. In fact, his doctrine of the soul in general helped to mold the subsequent Christian concept of mankind.

D. Success of Christianity

Christianity was a product of the Hellenistic-Roman age and environment, a time of transition and unrest. Like the mystery cults and religious philosophies, it was a religious alternative and emerged and developed to meet the needs of the time. The Jewish people had long awaited a messiah, and found him in the person and message of Jesus. As a product of the age, Christianity shared the soteriological goals and ethical concerns of the cults and religious philosophies. Unlike them, however, Christianity was regarded with suspicion by the Roman authorities for almost 300 years. It was often criticized by the pagan intellectuals, and its followers were persecuted. Nonetheless, Christianity survived, continued to spread and prosper, and by the early 4th century it succeeded in conquering the Roman Empire and supplanting the cults and philosophies. By this time, Christianity had become the most effectively organized and disciplined body within the empire, independent and self-sufficient. Constantine (306-337) realized the strength and influence of the Christians and, after the battle of Chrysopolis in 324 when he emerged victorious as the sole ruler of the empire, he recognized Christianity as an official religion of the empire and became its generous patron. Constantine's massive benefaction to Christianity increased its power and prestige. Thus began the defeat of Roman paganism and its gods and the christianization of the empire, which was complete by the end of the 4th century. In 380, the emperor Theodosius I (347-395) proclaimed Christianity the official religion of the empire, and in 391 closed the pagan temples and sanctuaries and prohibited all forms of pagan worship. This caused the cults to gradually disappear, and paganism in general began to collapse.

Much of Christianity's success is due to the social and psychological benefits that it offered its adherents and which were not found in either the cults or philosophies. An important factor was its openness. From the very beginning, Christianity was open to all without any restrictions, other than steadfastness to the faith and moral and ethical conduct. The cults tended to be secretive and exclusive and their initiation rites often expensive.[68] Mithraism, the most successful of the mystery religions, excluded women from its rites and benefits. Although the philosophical schools functioned much like religious communities, they required some degree of education and made salvation an intellectual accomplishment. Christianity's intransigence was also an important factor for its success. Its refusal to compromise or accept any alternative forms of worship was a source of strength. It gave to Christianity a concentration and a cohesive force that was lacking from paganism's fluidity. Both the cults and the philosophies tolerated other gods and were open to diversification. Moreover, as a persecuted sect, Christianity was forced to become a close-knit, organized, and disciplined community with its members bound together by a common rite, a community of life, and by their common danger. From its inception, the Christian community gave its members a true sense of belonging, a sense of security. This sense of community was not found in any corresponding group of cults or philosophies. The Christian community was concerned for every aspect of each member's life, and ready to give whatever assistance one needed in captivity or other distress. However, Christian charity and philanthropy were not confined only to its members,

68. See above, Chapter I B.

116

but were universal. Christians gave freely to the poor, the hungry, and the thirsty; they visited the sick and the imprisoned, and clothed those that had no clothing.[69] Christianity's sense of community and its universal charity were a major reason, if not the most important single reason, for its growth and subsequent victory over the empire.

69. Cf. Matt. 25:34-40.

Chapter V

GNOSTICISM

A. Nature of Gnosticism

Gnosticism was yet another religious movement of the Hellenistic-Roman age that offered a solution to the individual's search for *soteria* or "salvation," deliverance from the evils and suffering of the earthly life, and was based on *gnosis*. The term *gnosis* is a Greek word, a verbal noun of *gignoskein*, "to know," and is applicable to any type of apprehending or knowledge. To the various sects that came to be known as Gnostics or *Gnostikoi*, "those who know," *gnosis* was understood as an esoteric knowledge of the divine, the universe, and of themselves, their place in the world, and their destiny. This knowledge, itself perfect redemption, was mediated to the Gnostic through revelation or illumination either by a divine messenger, a savior figure who in the Christian sects was often understood as Christ, or through an esoteric sacred tradition, and released the Gnostic from the world of matter, its evil, and suffering. The Gnostic now understood his/her true nature and divine origin and the supreme divine being, because an individual's true self, his/her soul or spirit, is a part of the deity. Gnostic *gnosis* or knowledge is a transforming knowledge, and its immediate effect is salvation. By means of this knowledge, the Gnostic had undergone a spiritual regeneration. He/she could no longer be affected by earthly matters and was assured that his ultimate destiny was the soul's return to the divine world and union with the supreme being. Thus, the Gnostics understood themselves as a "chosen people," an elite group, above the materially minded or unenlightened masses. Only a few of the sects called themselves Gnostics, "the knowing ones." The term was applied by the Christian heresiologists of the 2nd century C.E. to all who claimed to possess a special esoteric knowledge.

The historical origins of the gnostic movement are still an unresolved question, but four main theories of its source prevail: Hellenistic philosophical thought, heterodox Judaism, Christianity, and Eastern religious thought — Egyptian, Syrian, Iranian, or Indian. Evidence of the gnostic movement first appeared in Christian writings of the 2nd century, and although some scholars have attempted to argue for an earlier pre-Christian Gnosticism, their evidence is conjectural. Some elements, beliefs, and tendencies incorporated in the various gnostic systems can be found in pre-Christian pagan and Jewish writings, but they are not gnostic in the strict sense of the word.[1] Like many of the other religious ideas of the Hellenistic-Roman age, Gnosticism was a phenomenon fostered by the ever transient conditions of the time and the continuing sufferings and misfortunes that created in individuals a sense of insecurity and alienation. In Gnosticism, the conditions of the time reached a particular intensity, a radicalism that led to a social and religious revolt. The Gnostics felt repelled and alienated from the world. They rejected the traditional views of the divine, the universe, and humanity's place and destiny in the world, and thus the governance of both the supernatural and visible world and its despots and rulers, and sought through *gnosis* to ascend to a world beyond, a world of freedom. *Gnosis* liberated them from the material world with its social and legal constraints. The Gnostics felt free to establish their own individual patterns and standards of behavior.[2] Thus, gnostic social and ethical conduct was either ascetic or libertine. Although extreme opposites, both expressed the same fundamental attitude, the rejection of and release from the conventional norms of behavior: asceticism through abstinence and libertinism through excess.[3]

Gnosticism was not a uniform religion, but an attitude about the universe and the individual manifested in a number of groups or sects within Judaism, Christianity, and paganism during the 2nd and 3rd centuries. The

1. For an excellent discussion of this point, see Arthur Darby Nock, "Gnosticism," *HTR* 57 (1964): 255-79.

2. Henry Alan Green, "Suggested Sociological Themes in the Study of Gnosticism," *VC* 31 (1977): 169-80.

3. Hans Jonas, *The Gnostic Religion,* 2nd ed. (Boston: Beacon, 1963), 270-77; Kurt Rudolph, *Gnosis: The Nature and History of Gnosticism* (San Francisco: Harper & Row, 1987), 252-57.

most important movement was Christian Gnosticism, which attempted to express Christianity in forms and concepts suitable to the scientific and philosophical understanding of the time. Christian Gnosticism was especially influential during the 2nd and 3rd centuries, when the various gnostic teachers dominated the Christian intellectual life, and each one promulgated his individual views. The movement was a product of Hellenistic philosophic-religious syncretism, an eclectic fusion of philosophical speculation, astrology, mythology, and Egyptian, Persian, Jewish Hellenistic, and Christian ideas. Until the 20th century, Gnosticism was considered a Christian heresy. The movement was known primarily from the works of Christian heresiologists of the 2nd and 3rd centuries. Recent scholarship and discoveries, however, have indicated that there also existed a pagan Gnosticism. The *Corpus Hermeticum,* written by various authors sometime in the 2nd or 3rd century, is of a pagan gnostic nature. Non-Christian gnostic documents were also found among the recently discovered Coptic library at Nag Hammadi, Egypt, in 1945. The Nag Hammadi codices, as the documents are known, consist of 13 Coptic books dating to the middle of the 4th century and believed to have been used by Christians. Although the writings are in Coptic, they are translations from Greek originals that many scholars claim were written sometime between the second half of the 1st century and the first half of the 2nd century.[4] The bulk of the material is gnostic, both Christian and non-Christian. There are also pieces of nongnostic material and some works that reflect Jewish traditions, apocalyptic and extrabiblical.[5]

The gnostic movement was multi-faceted. It took many forms, ranging from extreme speculation to the crudest fantasies. The Gnostics were organized into diverse groups led by an individual teacher who was frequently the founder of the community. There did not exist a gnostic church, canon, normative theology, or rule of faith. Thus, each community leader was free to present his/her mode of thought within the framework of the gnostic beliefs and understandings. There were numerous gnostic groups. The wide variety of names existing among the gnostic groups indicates the multiplicity of the movement's thought and activities. According to the early Christian fathers, the individual gnostic sects derived their

4. Elaine Pagels, *The Gnostic Gospels* (New York: Random House, 1979), XVI-XVII.
5. James M. Robinson, ed., *The Nag Hammadi Library in English*, 3rd ed. (San Francisco: Harper & Row, 1988), 7-9.

names from either their founders, their place of origin, or nationality, their activities or practices, their dominant doctrines, or the objects of their enthusiasm or worship.[6] It is not certain that they applied these names to themselves or were given to them by their opponents.[7] Although the gnostic sects were widely divergent and disunited, there existed among the various systems, both Christian and pagan, certain common concepts. Common to all was the unique understanding of *gnosis,* a revealed knowledge through which salvation is achieved. Other common understandings included the dualistic view of the world, the centrality of humankind in the world, and its salvation.

B. Main Tenets

One of the principal features of Gnosticism was its radical dualistic view of the world.[8] According to the Gnostics, there were two worlds, a purely spiritual, divine, invisible higher world of light and a material world of evil, darkness, and inevitable death. The spiritual world was the realm of the supreme God, the "Father of all," the ultimate cause of all things called by the Gnostics the "unknown God." This God is ineffable, indescribable, completely transcendent, free from any relationship to all that is visible or sensible, and incorporates a world of plenitude and divine perfection known as the Pleroma, a realm of heavenly beings or aeons. At some point, an aeon of the divine Pleroma fell from the realm of light. Depending on the gnostic system, the principal of the fall was either a male figure, a female hypostasis, or Sophia. The cause of the fall was usually ignorance and passion, and its result was the creation of the material world and humankind. Brought into existence by a fallen deity, the material world, which is a copy of the higher world, is an antithesis to the divine self-contained remote world of light; it is a realm of darkness and evil. In most of the gnos-

6. Robert M. Grant, *Gnosticism and Early Christianity,* rev. ed. (New York: Harper & Row, 1966), 6-7.

7. Robert M. Grant, 6-7.

8. Currently, a large amount of literature exists on Gnosticism, especially since the discovery of the *Nag Hammadi Codices* in 1945. The summary of Gnosticism's main tenets in this chapter is abstracted from the following texts: Giovanni Filoramo, *A History of Gnosticism* (Cambridge, Mass.: Blackwell, 1990); Robert Haardt, *Gnosis: Character and Testimony* (Leiden: E. J. Brill, 1971); Jonas; Pagels; Rudolph.

tic systems, the creator-god was known as the demiurge and often equated with the God of the Old Testament. The demiurge first created the evil powers, the archons or rulers, and then formed the cosmos. Generally, the archons consist of the seven planetary spheres and the 12 signs of the zodiac. Together, the demiurge and the archons rule over the world and each individual. Their rule, which is called *heimarmene,* "universal Fate or Destiny," is tyrannical and its purpose is the enslavement of humankind. The Gnostics viewed the material world as a disastrous accident. Everything that existed within it was a symbol of disorder and suffering. They rejected the world and its inferior creator, and considered as their only true God the Supreme unknown God. The Gnostic's aim was to free oneself from this world and to find one's place in the world of light with the true God.

The principal concern of the Gnostics was the individual and his/her salvation. They believed that the individual consisted of body, soul, and spirit. The body and soul are products of the demiurge and the archons, who formed the body and animated it by means of the soul with a share of their nature, the attributes peculiar to each planet. These include the appetites and passions of the individual. The spirit of the individual is a spark of the divine, supreme God, and is derived directly from him. It is the only part of an individual capable of attaining salvation. In most gnostic systems, the three basic elements — body, soul, and spirit — are present in each person in varying degrees. The element that predominates in each person determines the type of individual that he/she is and his/her destiny, and it is decided at birth. Thus, most of the gnostic groups divide humankind into three categories: the *pneumatikoi* or "spiritual," the *psychikoi* or "soul-like," and the *hylikoi,* the "material" or "earthly" individuals. The spirit predominates in the *pneumatikoi.* These individuals are the Gnostics and capable of redemption. They possess spiritual understanding and are able to respond to the divine element within them. The *psychikoi* possess soul and free will, but lack the enlightenment of the *pneumatikoi.* They cannot attain the highest level, a place in the Pleroma, but possessing free will, they are capable of choosing between good and evil. If they choose to follow the good and to live a life of good conduct, they can attain a lower heavenly realm. The *hylic* group is dominated by the carnal element and is spiritually ignorant. They are not even aware of the need for salvation, and thus have no hope of being saved.

The goal of the Gnostic is to understand his/her divine nature. By understanding one's divine nature, the Gnostic also understands God, of whom he/she is a spark, the nature of the world, and the purpose and destiny of humankind, and is thus saved. The Gnostic has been liberated from the bonds of the material world, the influence of fate, and the social and moral controls which, the Gnostics believed, were the domain of the evil demiurge and another form of cosmic tyranny. Thus, the Gnostic was assured of a place in the Pleroma, the realm of light, after death. Free from all worldly constraints, the Gnostics determined their own behavioral patterns. They showed their contempt and hostility for the precepts of the demiurge by a type of counter-existence. Some gnostic systems advocated a strict asceticism that minimized their contact with the world and thus prevented any further contamination by it. Other groups advocated antinomian libertinism, a deliberate defiance of the social and moral demands, both divine and human. By intentionally rejecting all law, the Gnostics believed that they thwarted the designs of the demiurge and his powers, the archons, and in a paradoxical way assisted in the work of salvation.[9]

For the Gnostics, complete liberation, a release from the bonds of the body, came at the death of the body. Death frees the spirit to return to its true home, the realm of light. Its return is long and arduous, and consists of the soul's ascent through the planetary spheres from which it had descended. In its ascent, the soul returns to each sphere the attribute that it received on its journey to earth. The governors of each sphere, the archons, try to impede the soul from ascending. To ward off or to overcome the obstacles of the archons, the soul requires help and support from concrete elements; *gnosis* is not sufficient. In most gnostic systems, the archons' menace was overcome by prayers recited by the dying or those caring for him, a special formula that the soul recites before each power on the ascent, magical sayings, or mysterious signs and symbols. Some late gnostic groups performed death ceremonies to assure the soul's passage without much difficulty. In some sects, this ceremony included the anointing of the dead or dying with oil and water. When the soul had passed successfully through the planetary spheres, the spirit was detached from the soul and entered the realm of light to reside with the true God. Gnostic eschatology was not restricted to the individual's return to the realm of light, but also included the end of the world. The Gnostics believed that the world had a beginning and will have an end. In most systems, the end of the world will

9. Jonas, 46.

occur when all particles of light, those which are capable of being liberated, have returned to the Pleroma, bringing about its restoration. With the reunification of the particles of light with the divine substance, the world is deprived of its light and is dissolved. According to the Gnostics, the end of the world is final, with no possibility of renewal.

C. Principal Gnostic Systems

Christian

It is thought that one of the causes for the rise of Christian Gnosticism was the delay of the Parousia, Christ's return. The early Christians eagerly awaited the imminent return of Christ, who would eliminate the evil and suffering in the world. By the 2nd century, the nonoccurrence of the Parousia caused a number of Christian teachers to present views of the world and mankind's escape from its oppression that deviated from the standard Christian beliefs. During the 2nd and 3rd centuries, a succession of gnostic teachers dominated Christian intellectual life. Gnostic sects and speculation were especially prominent in Alexandria and spread from there throughout the Christian world. The Christian heresiologists of the 2nd and 3rd centuries attributed the rise of Gnosticism to Simon Magus, a contemporary of the apostles and a convert to Christianity who is first mentioned in Acts 8:9-24. Although Simon Magus introduced the dualistic view of the world, he was not a true Gnostic. His views were basically heterodox Jewish and essentially monotheistic. Of the many gnostic sects that developed, the most important were those of Basilides (fl. ca. 130-150), Marcion (fl. 140-160), and Valentinus (fl. ca. 140-160). All three considered themselves Christians and claimed to preserve the true revelation of Christ.

Basilides

The first important Christian gnostic teacher was Basilides, who taught in Alexandria during the second quarter of the 2nd century. Almost nothing is known about his life or of his literary works. Only a few fragments of his writings survive; the titles of his literary output are preserved in the works of Clement of Alexandria, Origen, and Hegemonius, who wrote a polemic against heretics sometime during the second quarter of the 4th century.[10] Eusebius (ca. 260–ca. 339) attributes to Basilides a 24-book biblical commentary, the *Exegetica*,[11] and Origen claims that he wrote a book of *Odes*.[12] The heresiologists Irenaeus of Lyons (ca. 115–ca. 202) and Hippolytus of Rome (ca. 170–ca. 236) present two very different accounts of Basilides' thought. Scholars generally agree that Hippolytus's account is the more accurate. Irenaeus's version is thought to be a later development of Basilides' teaching that was taught by his followers.

Hippolytus[13] presents Basilides' thinking as essentially monistic, according to which in the beginning there was nothing, not even God. Accordingly, Basilides stresses God's indescribability: God is beyond any description. Since no statement could be made about the deity, Basilides calls him nonexistent. The nonexistent God brought forth, without violation, a world-seed, from which everything that exists proceeds. In the world-seed were three principles known as "sonships," consubstantial with the nonexistent God. The first, the most light and subtle, immediately returned to God; the second, more opaque, was unable to ascend on its own and provided itself with wings, which Basilides calls the Holy Spirit. When the second sonship returned to God, it left its wings, the Holy Spirit, behind as a type of firmament, the space between the upper and lower worlds. The third sonship was too heavy to rise; he needed purification and remained in the lower world to practice and benefit by good deeds. This sonship represents the spiritual substance, the souls in the material world in need of purification and salvation. After the sonships, the world-seed produced two archons or demiurges. The first was charged with the creation of the Ogdoad, the realm of the fixed stars; the second, with the creation of the Hebdomad, the world below the stars. This latter archon, according to Basilides, was the god of Abraham, Isaac, and Jacob.

After the creation of the entire world, the gospel, which represents *gnosis*, the knowledge of the spiritual world, of creation, and its destiny, came into the world like a ray of light. It passed through each realm, prin-

---

10. A collection of the fragments in English is found in Bentley Layton, *The Gnostic Scriptures* (Garden City: Doubleday, 1987), 427-44.

11. *Hist. eccl.* 4.7.7.

12. *Ennarat. Job* 21.11.

13. Hippolytus's account is from his *Refutatio omnium haeresium* 7.20-27, ed. by Paul Wendland, Die Griechischen Christlichen Schriftsteller der Ersten Drei Jahrhunderte 3 (Leipzig: J. C. Hinrichs, 1916); for an English translation, see Haardt, 41-55.

cipality, and power, instructing and enlightening them. Then it descended into Mary and became incarnated in Jesus. Jesus' life and suffering was for the purpose of leading back to the spiritual world above the cosmos the divine elements in the lower world, the spiritual beings or pneumatics, represented by the third sonship. When they have all returned, the nonexistent God will bring a cosmic ignorance over the whole world. The souls that remain below will neither be saved nor be aware of the need for salvation. They will remain in accordance with their nature and will not strive for anything that is counter to it. Basilides' pessimistic eschatology is more extreme than in any other gnostic system and expresses his primary emphasis, humankind's hopeless state on earth, and the possibility of salvation through Jesus.

Irenaeus's[14] description of Basilides' system is less detailed and more dualistic. He does not mention the world-seed, but describes the universe as a series of successive emanations that are derived from the nonexistent God. The first emanations or aeons consist of *Nous* (mind or Christ), *Logos* (word), *Pronesis* (prudence), *Sophia* (wisdom), and *Dynamis* (power), and constitute the divine world or Pleroma. *Sophia* and *Dynamis* engendered 365 angelic powers in an unbroken descending order. Each of these in turn created a heaven on the model of the preceding. These 365 heavens correspond to the earthly year and also symbolize the great distance between God and the created world. The angels in the last heaven, the one visible to humans, created the material world and humankind. Their ruler is Yahweh, the God of the Jews, whose aim was to bring all nations under the rule of the Jews. The rulers of the other nations resisted, and a continual struggle for predominance ensued, causing the evils that afflict the world and its people. In order to deliver humankind from the oppression of the Jewish God and his powers, the supreme, nonexistent God sent his *Nous*, called Christ, to liberate all those who believed in him from the power of the angels who had created the world. Christ appeared in the form of a man named Jesus. Before the crucifixion, he exchanged roles with Simon of Cyrene. Thus, it was not Jesus who was crucified but Simon. Jesus, unharmed, ascended to the one who had sent him, the nonexistent God. Anyone who acknowledges the man who was crucified, Simon, remains a slave

---

14. The description is from Irenaeus's *Adversus haereses* 1.24.3-7, ed. by W. W. Harvey (Cambridge: Cambridge University Press, 1857); for an English translation, see Layton, 422-25.

to the demiurgic powers, while anyone who follows the *Nous* or Christ is free and has knowledge of the nonexistent's providential plans. Of the individuals who attain salvation, only their spirit is saved. The body is the product of the demiurgic powers and is corruptible.

Marcion

The idea of the nonexistent or unknowable supreme God and the subordination of the creator God was also adopted and developed by Marcion, a contemporary of Basilides. Information about Marcion's life and work is derived exclusively from his opponents and primarily from Irenaeus, Hippolytus, and Tertullian.[15] Marcion was born in Sinope, a port on the Black Sea, ca. 85 C.E., the son of a prosperous ship owner who also served as bishop of the local Christian community. Ca. 139/40, he went to Rome and became a prominent member of the Roman church, but soon came under the influence of Cerdo, a Syrian gnostic teacher, whose ideas he developed. Principal among Cerdo's views was the concept of two Gods, the supreme unknowable God and the Creator God of the Old Testament, and their antithesis.[16] In 144, Marcion attempted to expound this view to the leaders of the Roman church in a synod and was excommunicated. Unlike other gnostic teachers, Marcion proceeded to found a church. In general, gnostic groups organized as schools in which the teachings were transmitted, interpreted, and kept secret. Marcion was the first Gnostic to establish a church with an organization, liturgy, and Scripture that was very similar to that of the church of Rome. He was also the first to develop a New Testament canon, which included an abridged version of the Gospel of Luke and a modified version of the 10 Pauline letters. The Pastoral Epistles (1, 2 Timothy, and Titus) and the Epistle to the Hebrews were excluded.

Marcion's doctrine advocated the existence of two Gods who have nothing in common. One is the unknowable supreme God who is good and merciful and the Father of Jesus Christ, and the other is the God of creation, the demiurge of the cosmos and subordinate to the superior God. In a work now lost, the *Antitheses*, Marcion systematically presents point

---

15. The most extensive discussion of Marcion's life and work is found in Tertullian's 5-volume work *Adversus Marcionem (Against Marcion)*, ed. and trans. by Ernest Evans (Oxford: Clarendon, 1972).

16. Irenaeus *Haer.* 1.27.1-2; 4.17.11; Tertullian *Marc.* 1.2; 2.24.

by point the difference between the two Gods. The God of creation and ruler of the world is the Old Testament God. He is the known God, known from his creation that reveals not only his existence, but also his character. The imperfection, vindictiveness, and inconsistency in the world reflect those of the demiurge. Marcion claims that it is the Creator God that is responsible for the world's misfortune, evil, and death. According to Marcion, the Creator God is just, ruling according to the justice of the Old Testament, which Marcion understood as retaliatory and vindictive. He administers justice according to everyone's deserts, but he is without mercy, even to his own people, the Jews, as demonstrated by his actions described in the Old Testament.[17] In contrast to him is the supreme unknowable God who is revealed only in the gospel.[18] He is a good God, but alien since he was not involved or concerned with the creation of the world and humankind. His only intervention in the created world was an act of unfathomable love and goodness.[19] The alien God who had no preexisting relation or obligation to the human race, who are beings of another God, had mercy for these beings and sent his son Jesus Christ to liberate them from the bonds of the world and its creator through his own suffering.[20]

The Christ sent by the superior God is not the one prophesied in the Old Testament. Marcion believed that the Jewish Messiah will come at some future time to restore the Jewish kingdom just as the prophets declared, but he has nothing to do with humankind's salvation.[21] The Christ sent by the unknown God is a different being and was sent to save the souls that Marcion called "the inner man" of all humankind.[22] Christ was revealed in the 15th year of the reign of Tiberius "as a man but not a man"; his body was only a "phantasm."[23] Marcion's hostility to matter caused him to deny Christ's human birth.[24] In this "phantasm" body he was crucified and descended into Hades, where he ransomed the souls of those who are condemned in the Old Testament, while those who had been justified by the Creator God remained unredeemed. The latter, knowing from expe-

---

17. Tertullian *Marc.* 1.2; 2.18-1, 23; 4.16, 23.

18. *Marc.* 4.16.

19. *Marc.* 1.17, 27.

20. *Marc.* 1.14.

21. *Marc.* 4.6.

22. Hippolytus *Haer.* 10.19; Tertullian *Marc.* 3.21.1.

23. Tertullian *Marc.* 3.8; 4.6-7.

24. *Marc.* 1.14.

rience that their God was forever tempting them, assumed that he was tempting them once again and did not believe him and thus remained in Hades.[25] Whoever believes in Christ is released from the bonds of the law and the censures and malice of the Creator God and is free to live a new life.[26] This new life was one of trust and faith in Christ and of strict asceticism that included minimal contact with the created order to avoid further contamination.

The purpose of Marcion's asceticism was not for spiritual sanctification, but the rejection of the created and worldly things. By refusing to employ what the creator God made or instituted, Marcion and his followers believed that they were annoying the demiurge and hindering his work.[27] Thus Marcion advocated abstinence from meat and wine, the temptations of the world, and especially abstinence from marriage and procreation. Procreation was a means of using, populating, and perpetuating the Creator God's world against which Marcion and his followers were rebelling and attempting to escape.[28] Marcion understood Christ's salvation to be a physical rather that a spiritual one, the freeing or liberation of humankind from the confinement, misery, and suffering of its environment. Those who believe and trust in Christ and live an ascetic life will, one day, be resurrected "in the soul." The body being material perishes and does not rise again.[29]

Marcion's Gnosticism is not typical of the movement of his time, especially his concept of the individual's nature and his salvation, so that many scholars have questioned whether he actually was a Gnostic. Unlike for his gnostic contemporaries, humankind in Marcion's anthropology does not participate in the divine essence. Both the individual's body and soul were created by the demiurge and share in his imperfection. All of humankind, through an act of incomprehensible kindness of the supreme God, is capable of salvation, not only a few, the *pneumatikoi*, as in other gnostic systems. In Marcion's system, although humankind is completely dependent on the superior God's goodness and mercy, God remains forever unknown to the created beings. Salvation is attained through faith and belief in Christ and not through a revealed *gnosis*. The saved are be-

25. Irenaeus *Haer.* 1.27.3.
26. Tertullian *Marc.* 1.17, 22.
27. Hippolytus *Haer.* 10.19.
28. Clement *Strom.* 3.4.25; Tertullian *Marc.* 1.29.
29. Tertullian *Marc.* 1.24; Irenaeus *Haer.* 1.27.3.

lievers, not "knowers." Marcion's view of salvation is closer to that of Pauline Christianity than to Gnosticism, but the anti-cosmic dualism that he vigorously stressed identifies him as very much a Gnostic. Like many during that time and especially the Gnostics, Marcion was obsessed with the question of the origin of evil, which was attributed to the unmanageable nature of matter and its creator.[30] He rejected the Creator God of the Old Testament, his words and works, and postulated a superior God who was opposed to the created world. Since Marcion considered matter evil, he denied the humanity of Jesus and the resurrection of the body. These views were quite prevalent in 2nd-century gnostic thought.

Marcion considered the Old Testament irrelevant to Christianity, and his principal aim was to separate the law from the gospel.[31] This he attempted to accomplish in the *Antitheses,* in which he contrasted statements from the Old and the New Testaments, arranged in a way to substantiate the diversity between them.[32] He rejected the typological and allegorical interpretation of the Scriptures, and interpreted each verse literally in an attempt to prove the incompatibility of the two Scriptures and the irreconcilable differences between the words and deeds of the superior God and those of the Creator God.[33] Although he did not accept the Old Testament as a Christian Scripture, Marcion considered it an important and reliable historical account of the history of mankind, and in particular of the Jewish race.

Concerning the New Testament, Marcion accepted the Epistles of Paul (but not the Pastorals and Hebrews) and the Gospel of Luke. He believed that of all the apostles, only Paul understood Jesus' message correctly, and it was Paul who had received the authentic gospel by revelation. Luke's Gospel was accepted because Marcion understood Luke to be a companion of Paul's and that he was influenced by him. The other Gospels he considered Judaic forgeries.[34] Even Luke's Gospel and the Pauline Epistles had

---

30. *Marc.* 1.2.

31. *Marc.* 1.19.

32. *Marc.* 4.1. Marcion's *Antitheses* is lost. What remains of the work was reconstructed by Adolf von Harnack, *Marcion: Das Evangelium vom fremden Gott,* 2nd ed. (Leipzig: J. C. Hinrichs, 1924), App. V; Eng. trans., *Marcion: The Gospel of the Alien God,* by John E. Steely and Lyle D. Bierma (Durham, N.C.: Labyrinth, 1990). The extant parts are also found in Tertullian *Marc.,* esp. 1-3.

33. *Marc.* 4.6.

34. *Marc.* 4.3.

been adulterated by the Judaists, and Marcion felt obligated to restore them to their authentic form and content. He edited the works and removed all judaizing interpolations. All quotations from the Old Testament were removed, all references of Christ's relationship with the Creator God, and his fulfillment of Old Testament prophecies. From Luke he also omitted Jesus' nativity, his baptism, his Jewish genealogy, his temptation, and his postresurrection appearances.[35]

Marcion was a formidable foe of Christianity and one of its few opponents to be condemned by all theologians, Greek and Latin. Unlike other gnostic teachers, he was an arduous missionary and traveled throughout the Hellenistic-Roman world establishing churches in an attempt to convince the world to accept the authentic gospel and return to true Christianity.[36] During the second half of the 2nd century, Marcion's churches were found throughout the "whole world."[37] These churches were organized hierarchically, and in their sacramental teaching retained the sacrament of the Eucharist (except that water was used instead of wine) and the sacrament of baptism.[38] They baptized in the name of the Trinity,[39] but baptism was permitted only to those individuals who were willing to give up everything in the world, including family life, and to follow the strict ascetic principles that Marcion advocated.[40] However, by the 3rd century, Marcion's influence was beginning to diminish. It is thought that this was due in large part to the severe ascetic practices of the sect and to Marcion's totally indefensible understanding of Christ.[41] A century later, during the 4th century, Marcionism was absorbed into the Manichaean sect.

Valentinus

Another influential Gnostic of the 2nd century, and often considered the most influential, was the Christian teacher Valentinus. He was born and

35. Marcion's significant omissions and emendations are found in App. 2 of Evans's edition of Tertullian's *Marcion*.

36. *Marc.* 4.5.

37. *Marc.* 5.19.

38. *Marc.* 1.14.

39. For a discussion of Marcion's use of the trinitarian formula, see Edwin C. Blackman, *Marcion and his Influence* (London: SPCK, 1948), App. 3.

40. *Marc.* 4.11.

41. *Marc.* 1.27.

educated in Alexandria. Sometime in 140, he went to Rome as a Christian teacher and was quite successful. Valentinus was nominated for a bishopric, but was passed over in favor of Pius the Martyr. Soon after, he broke with the Christian community and was later considered a heretic.[42] Little more is known of Valentinus or of his work, of which only a few fragments are extant, preserved mainly by Clement of Alexandria. The fragments are primarily homilies, hymns, and letters, but they are not sufficient to reconstruct a system of thought.[43] Valentinus's writings were considered to be works of great artistry and were admired even by his opponents.[44] Information about Valentinian thought is derived from the theological systems developed by his numerous students, many of whom were influential in the spread and development of Gnosticism. They were heads of gnostic schools and teachers of their own form of Valentinianism. Until the discovery of the Nag Hammadi corpus, knowledge of the system was derived from the works of the Christian heresiologists, who present six different versions.[45] The Nag Hammadi corpus includes four works that share certain common ideas that are believed to have also been held by Valentinus.[46]

Common to all Valentinians was the idea of God as a single, totally unknowable, and incomprehensible being. The divine world or Pleroma consists of 30 aeons or spiritual beings arranged in pairs, or *syzygiae.* The first four pairs are the most important and form the primordial Ogdoad, from which all the other aeons originate. These are called *Bythos,* Primal Cause or Depth, who is the head of the whole system; *Sige,* Silence; *Nous,* Understanding; *Aletheia,* Truth; *Logos,* Rational Faculty; *Zoe,* Life; *Anthropos,* Human Being; and *Ekklesia,* Church. The last aeon to be produced was *Sophia,* Wisdom. She was the farthest away from the primal cause or Bythos and the weakest. As such, she is said to be "lacking" and filled with "revolt." From this emotion or "error" arose the whole of the

42. Tertullian *Adversus Valentinanos* 4, ed. by A. Kroyman, Corpus Scriptorum Ecclesiasticorum Latinorum 47 (Leipzig: G. Freytag, 1906).

43. A collection of the fragments is found in Layton, 229-48.

44. Clement *Strom.* 7.17.106.

45. The heresiologists include Irenaeus, Hippolytus, Clement of Alexandria, Origen, Tertullian, and Epiphanius.

46. The works are found in *NHL* and include the *Gospel of Truth,* 34-51; *Treatise on the Resurrection to Rheginus,* 52-57; *Gospel of Philip,* 139-60; and *Exegesis on the Soul,* 190-98. For a reconstruction of Valentinus's thought see Layton, 223-27.

material world. For her error, Sophia was separated from the Pleroma by *Horos,* a boundary, but she did not lose her divine origin. Outside of the Pleroma, Sophia brought forth a child who is the demiurge or creator-god, and ruler of all the material world. In order to redeem Sophia, Jesus and the Holy Spirit were sent from the divine realm. Through knowledge, they enlightened her and separated her from her error or ignorance. This established the process of salvation in the created world, the restoration of the fallen spiritual element that the Gnostics possess, to the divine Pleroma.

Similar to other gnostic schools, the Valentinians divided mankind into three classes, the *hylikoi,* the *psychikoi,* and the *pneumatikoi.* The purpose of the *pneumatikoi* is to perfect their knowledge of God through *gnosis* and to ascend again to the Pleroma. When all the *pneumatikoi* are perfected, the world will come to an end. At that time, the *pneumatikoi,* as pure spirits, will return to the divine Pleroma and will be presented as brides to the angels who are with the Savior. The souls of the *psychikoi* who have lived a righteous life along with the demiurge will attain partial salvation. They can not enter the Pleroma, but will find repose in the "place of the Middle," which lies between the Ogdoad and the created world.[47] The *hylikoi* will pass into nonexistence, consumed by the fire that is hidden in the world and will blaze forth and consume all matter.[48]

Valentinus's many disciples freely attempted to improve the work of the master, as is evidenced by the many different accounts of his system, so that by the late 2nd and early 3rd centuries the school had divided into two branches. The Anatolian or oriental branch was active in Egypt, Syria, and Asia Minor, and the Italian branch was dominant in Rome and spread as far as Southern Gaul. According to the heresiologist Hippolytus,[49] the main point of contention between the two schools concerned the body of Jesus. The Anatolians attributed a pneumatic or spiritual body to Jesus from the time of his birth, while the Italians claimed that he had a psychic body and that he received the spirit or logos at the time of his baptism. The Valentinian system with its numerous and important followers was long-lived. Records from the end of the 7th century make reference to the Valentinians.

47. Irenaeus *Haer.* 1.6.1.
48. Irenaeus *Haer.* 1.7.1.
49. Hippolytus *Haer.* 6.35.5-7.

Non-Christian

Of the non-Christian gnostic literature extant, the most important is the *Corpus Hermeticum* or *Hermetica,* a collection of separate treatises that are considered the divine revelation of Hermes Trismegistos, "Hermes the Thrice-great." Hermes is the Greek designation of the Egyptian god Thoth, who was believed to be the scribe of the gods, the inventor of writing, and patron of the arts and sciences. The works were written in Greek sometime during the 2nd and 3rd centuries, and are a part of an extensive literature of a pagan gnostical nature. They were produced in Egypt and represent the general Greco-Egyptian religious philosophy of the time, and include astrological, magical, mythological, and mystical material. Some also reveal influence from the Septuagint. The writings are of various anonymous authorship and of divergent views, sometimes even in a single tractate.[50] Nonetheless, there is a similarity among them. They all present a syncretistic religious philosophy that is a divine revelation and capable of being taught. One of the principal treatises of the corpus, and the one that best expresses the Hermetic view of God, the world, the individual, and the attainment of salvation, is the *Poimandres.* The work is also an important source of pagan gnostic cosmogony and anthropogeny. It is an eclectic fusion of Septuagint, Jewish-Hellenistic, Stoic, Neo-Pythagorean, and Platonic views, primarily the Platonic views found in the *Timaeus,* expressed in the form of divine revelation.

The general philosophical basis of the *Poimandres* shows affinity with Middle Platonic thought, especially that of Numenius, with which it was contemporary. However, there is no evidence in the treatise of a direct dependence on Numenius, or conversely that Numenius was influenced by the *Poimandres.* In its treatment of traditional Hebrew material, there are numerous verbal and conceptual affinities with Philo. As with Numenius, there is no reason to suppose any dependence on Philo's works. Rather, the affinities are considered by scholars to be parallel developments from a similar religious-philosophical environment.

The meaning of the term "Poimandres" is not known, but some schol-

---

50. E.g., *Corp. herm.* 10.7-8 as opposed to 19. The text of the *Hermetica* used in this study is from the edition of A. D. Nock and A.-J. Festugière, *Corpus Hermeticum* 1-4 (Paris: Les Belles Lettres, 1945-1954); Greek text and French translation. An English translation is found in Haardt, 167-76.

ars deduce that it is from the Coptic *p-eime-n-re*, "the knowledge of the Sun-god."[51] The work is an autobiography and relates the experience of an unnamed man, understood to be Hermes Trismegistos, who desired to know the nature of all that exists. Thereupon he had a vision in which the divine supreme intellect, the archetypal Nous or God, revealed to him the divine origin of the universe and of mankind, and he was taught, through divine revelation, the way of the soul's deliverance and return to its immortal and divine state. After he had been taught the truth about the things that exist, Hermes is instructed to teach others the doctrine of salvation that had been revealed to him. The treatise ends with a hymn of thanks to God.[52] Unlike many of the contemporary gnostic schools, the *Poimandres* does not divide humankind into different classes with varying capabilities of salvation. All individuals can be saved if they are willing to attain the necessary *gnosis* or knowledge.

According to the *Poimandres*, God is one, simple, incorporeal, ineffable, immaterial, infinite, transcendent, and eternal, existing before all creation — from all eternity.[53] He is the Supreme Mind, the Absolute Sovereignty, the Father of all, the source of all being and reason.[54] Within God, existing with him from all eternity, are innumerable powers arranged in a limitless cosmos. These powers are the intelligible archetypal world forms comprising the intelligible world, and are analogous to the Platonic world of ideas.[55] From the Supreme Mind issued forth a second divine being, the Logos or thought of God, for the purpose of differentiating and ordering the chaotic primal matter.[56] The chaotic matter had a beginning, but an account of its origin is not given.[57] Issuing from the divine Mind, the Logos is considered an offspring of God or son of God, of the same essence and inseparable from him.[58] The Logos assailed and permeated the dark, chaotic,

51. C. H. Dodd, *The Bible and the Greeks* (London: Hodder & Stoughton, 1935), 67.

52. A similar view of salvation is found in *Corp. herm.* XIII and the Hermetic treatise in *NHL*, VI.6.

53. *Corp. herm.* 1.6, 8. A discussion of the *Poimandres* is found in Antonía Tripolitis, *The Doctrine of the Soul* (Roslyn Heights, N.Y.: Libra, 1978), 17-23, and is the basis for the explanation in this study.

54. *Corp. herm.* 1.2, 12.

55. *Corp. herm.* 1.7, 8.

56. *Corp. herm.* 1.5, 8.

57. *Corp. herm.* 1.4.

58. *Corp. herm.* 1.6. For Logos as son of God, cf. Philo, *Migr.* 18.103; *Post.* 18.63; *Conf.* 14.63.

undifferentiated primal matter or raw material out of which the visible universe was made.[59] He caused the inchoate nature to separate into higher (fire, air) and lower (earth, water) elements, and hovered above the lower elements, keeping them in motion and in order.[60] Having brought forth the elements and in accordance with God's counsel, the Logos imitated the perfect archetypal world and constructed the sensible world.[61]

After the elements had been formed and ordered, God, an androgynous, generative principle that exists as Life and Light, generated another divine mind, the creator Mind or demiurge. The demiurge of the *Poimandres* does not have the negative qualities of other gnostic creators. He is neither ignorant nor malicious. Generated by God, he is God's offspring and as such is like the Father, both mind and god.[62] The demiurge is the God of Fire and *Pneuma* or ether, from which he created seven ruling powers or administrators, the seven planets.[63] These seven planetary gods encircle the sensible universe and administer it. Their rule is called *heimarmene*, Fate or Destiny.[64] With the establishment of the planetary spheres, the Logos departed from the sublunar world, ascended to the heavens and united with the demiurge, with whom he shared the same essence.[65]

The demiurge with the Logos, now one being, imparts a rotary motion to the planets, which causes, in accordance with God's will, the elements of the sublunar work — air, earth, and water — to produce the irrational beings that exist in the air, in the water, and on the earth.[66] Thus, although the *Poimandres* speaks of the Logos as a separate distinct entity, it is the formative creative power of the demiurge. It was generated for the purpose of differentiating undifferentiated chaos, but when this task was completed, the Logos fused and became one with the demiurge. From that

59. *Corp. herm.* 1.4, 5.

60. *Corp. herm.* 1.5; cf. 10.

61. *Corp. herm.* 1.5, 8. The cosmogony of the *Poimandres* is based on the Septuagint Genesis account of creation, interpreted philosophically. For parallels between the cosmogony of the treatise and Genesis, see Dodd, 99-144.

62. *Corp. herm.* 1.9; cf. 10, where the Logos is claimed to share the same essence as the Demiurge.

63. *Corp. herm.* 1.9, 16. *Pneuma* in this context seems to refer to ether, the fiery substance of the upper regions of the universe, the heavens, as opposed to the air or atmosphere of the lower or sublunar region. Cf. *Corp. herm.* 1.5, 11.

64. *Corp. herm.* 1.9.

65. *Corp. herm.* 1.10.

66. *Corp. herm.* 1.11. Cf. Philo *Opif.* 24.73 ff.; Gen. 1:24.

point onward, the Logos and demiurge are one being, concerned with the creation, ordering, and governing of the whole universe.[67]

Following the biblical account of creation, the treatise states that mankind was brought forth after the establishment of the cosmic order by the supreme God himself; but mankind was not created, being instead generated in a manner similar to that of the demiurge. Archetypal Man, *Anthropos* or Human Being whom God begot, bears the image of God and is considered a sibling of the demiurge, the third divine emanation of the supreme Mind, and hence pure mind. As such, mankind is incorporeal, immaterial, immortal, and divine.[68] Mankind was begotten out of God's desire to enjoy his own perfection in a perfect image of himself, one untouched by the admixture of the lower universe. God loved Man as his own child and gave to him complete mastery over his creation.[69] When Man observed the creation of his brother, the demiurge, he wished to create something himself. God granted him permission, and Man left the intelligible universe and entered the demiurgic sphere, the sphere of the seven planets. The planets became enamored of him, and each gave him a share of its nature, the disposition and quality peculiar to each. These form the irrational faculties or powers of the embodied individual, which clothe or envelop the rational mind as it descends through the spheres.[70] From the first sphere, Man received the disposition of deceitfulness; from the second, the evil desire for wealth; from the third, the impious audacity and the rashness of recklessness; from the fourth, the overbearing arrogance; from the fifth, the deceit of the passions; from the sixth, the contrivance of evil; and from the seventh, the power to grow and to decrease.[71] When he reached the seventh sphere, Man wished to break through the bounds of their orbits and looked down into *Physis,* the lower nature. Nature, when it saw that Man possessed all the energy of the ruling powers, the seven planets, and the form of God, smiled at him with love. Man, in turn, saw his reflection in the lower nature or matter, became enamored of it, descended into it, and became incarnated.[72]

---

67. *Corp. herm.* 1.10-11.

68. *Corp. herm.* 1.12-13; cf. 1.21.

69. *Corp. herm.* 1.12. Cf. Gen. 1:26-28.

70. The descent and return of the soul through the spheres is also found in the thought of Numenius (see above, 43) and in Mithraism (54-55).

71. *Corp. herm.* 1.13; cf. 1.25, where the account is given in inverse direction.

72. *Corp. herm.* 1.14.

As a result of primordial Man's fall, which was due to his love for matter, or more precisely his narcissism, human beings are of a dual nature, mortal and immortal. They consist of Light and Life, the essence of God from which primordial Man was formed and which in humans is intellect or mind and soul. The Light is mind and is the true or "essential" self; the soul is Life and unites the mind with the body. It is the sum of the accretions acquired by primordial Man on his descent through the planetary spheres, and serves as the center of free will. The body is a product of nature and is mortal.[73] Although humans are immortal as regards their divine nature and have authority over all things, they suffer the fate of mortals, since they are subject to Destiny, the power that governs the sensible world.[74] It is to the true self that each individual must strive to return. This is achieved through self-knowledge or understanding, when an individual realizes and recognizes his immortal, divine nature. Self-knowledge is knowledge of God, from whom the human race is derived. It leads an individual to realize the insignificance of all that is material and the evil effects of the love of the body, and causes the individual to shun the activities of the senses and to devote oneself to the love, devotion, and contemplation of God.[75] As an individual attains understanding, he advances towards God, who reveals himself to him and guides him to understand the things of nature and of the divine, to subdue the senses, ward off their influences and distractions, and escape the influence of Destiny.[76] According to the *Poimandres*, it is possible for an individual of advanced spiritual progress, on a rare occasion, and in a state of silent contemplation and yearning for knowledge of the divine, to arrive at a state of ecstasy and for a brief moment to attain a vision and union with the supreme Mind, even in this life. In this state, the senses are completely suppressed; the mind is liberated from the body temporarily and is illuminated by God. Man becomes totally pure mind and one with the supreme Mind.[77] Those individuals who are divinely inspired have the responsibility to guide and teach others the way back to God.[78]

73. *Corp. herm.* 1.17, 21; cf. 24-25. In the *Poimandres*, "mind" is used to refer to the transcendent, supra-cosmic element of man, while "soul" refers to his irrational part.

74. *Corp. herm.* 1.15.

75. *Corp. herm.* 1.18, 19-22.

76. *Corp. herm.* 1.21-22.

77. *Corp. herm.* 1.1, 4, 27, 30.

78. *Corp. herm.* 1.26; cf. 27, 32.

At the death and dissolution of the body, the righteous individual or soul ascends through the planetary spheres and returns to each sphere the irrational faculty or passion that it had received on its descent. Purified, pure mind, stripped of all its worldly encumbrances, it enters the eighth sphere, that of the fixed stars. There, together with the other pure beings, the purified mind exalts God and ascends beyond the eighth sphere to the intelligible universe, becomes one of the divine powers, enters into the vision of God, and becomes one with God, immortal and divine.[79] "This is the final good for those who have acquired *gnosis,* knowledge: to be deified."[80] The ascent of the soul through the spheres should not be understood literally. It is a description used metaphorically to represent an individual's progressive stages of spiritual purification that are anticipated here on earth while the soul is still in the material body.[81] There is no mention in the treatise of reincarnation of the disembodied, completely divinized individual. Therefore, union with God after the death of the body appears to be a permanent state for the righteous.

The individuals who minister to the body and surrender themselves to its senses live in ignorance and hence in sin. They live in a state of drunken sleep, in which the mind is dormant and the individual lives wholly by the bodily senses. These individuals are abandoned by God and are left prey to Destiny's rule, to the evil passions whose insatiability is their torment and who continue to increase in strength consuming them even more, and to the chastisements of their conscience.[82] The chastisement of the unrighteous continues even after the death of the body, and they forfeit their hope of immortality forever.[83] What becomes of these individuals after the death of the material body is not stated in the treatise, but it may be inferred that they break up into the elements of which they were composed and cease to exist as individuals.[84]

---

79. *Corp. herm.* 1.24-26. No clear explanation is given of the divine powers in par. 26, but they appear to be the same as those in par. 7 and 8, the intelligible archetypal world forms. See above, 137.

80. *Corp. herm.* 1.26.

81. Cf. esp. *Corp. herm.* 1.19 and 22.

82. *Corp. herm.* 1.19-20, 23; cf. 27.

83. *Corp. herm.* 1.19-20, 28.

84. Cf. *Corp. herm.* 1.23-24.

D. Gnosticism's Initial Appeal and Its Disappearance

Gnosticism was a movement of the middle years of the 2nd century that attempted to answer in a series of imaginative mythological, quasi-philo-sophical structures the questions that occupied the minds of many during that time — the nature of the divine, the universe, and humankind and its place in the world. In particular, it attempted to answer the question of the origin of evil. The movement was especially appealing to the Christian in-tellectuals, particularly those in Alexandria, to whom the 3rd-century theologian Origen credits its success.[85] By the end of the 2nd century, Gnosticism had become a worldwide movement and a formidable foe to Christianity. Its members were an "elect" group who claimed to possess a secret knowledge or *gnosis* not available to the rest of the populace. This claim had a psychological appeal. It gave the Gnostics a sense of security in an insecure world, and a sense of superiority. Through *gnosis,* they were re-leased from the rule of Fate or Destiny, with its suffering and enslavement, and they knew that no matter what occurred, they would survive and that their ultimate destiny was union with the supreme Deity.

For the ordinary individual who was seeking solutions to the prob-lems of human existence, Gnosticism did not provide adequate answers. Although the Gnostics attempted to offer solutions to the concerns of the time, their solutions were extreme and contrary to the traditional views of the world and humanity's place and destiny in it. The Gnostics were too hostile to the world; they viewed it as a place of evil and suffer-ing, and rejected it and its governance. They also rejected the human body as evil and negated the importance of human existence. Some Gnostics expressed their hostility to the world by advocating an austere and ascetic way of life, and others by accepting an extreme anti-nomianism. One of Gnosticism's main weaknesses, and a major factor in its disappearance, was its lack of organization. In general, the Gnostics remained individual secret schools. While Gnosticism advocated reli-gious individualism, orthodox Christianity was establishing an ecclesias-tical hierarchy. It was in the process of standardizing a scriptural canon based on apostolic authority, developing an authoritative formula of faith, a creed, and, unlike Gnosticism, was making attempts to come to terms with the social world in which it existed. Orthodox Christianity's

85. *Cels.* 3.12.

institutionalization was a major factor in Gnosticism's demise during the 4th century.

Gnosticism did, however, leave its imprint on Christianity. Its influence is evident in Christian mysticism and asceticism. The Gnostics' fanciful speculation of the divine nature forced Christian theologians to define clearly Christianity's christological and trinitarian doctrines. Their development of theological systems encouraged the Christians to formulate their own, in which they attempted to answer the questions posed by the Gnostics on the origin of evil in relation to the world and the individual. The gnostic concept of the spiritual individual or "inner man" influenced the Christian concept of humankind, its origin, its nature, and its return by means of knowledge to unity with its divine source.[86]

86. This is evident in the thought of Origen, the first Christian theologian to present a systematic concept of the individual soul. See above, 111-13.

Chapter VI

SUMMARY

Alexander's conquest, his cosmopolitan vision of a world community united by a common Greek language and culture, and a new cosmology altered forever peoples' view of the world, the divine, and themselves. His empire brought together Greek and oriental, Western and Eastern traditions and beliefs into a culturally unified Hellenistic world, as it came to be known. Provincialism was replaced by universalism, and collectivism by individualism. Individuals no longer identified with a particular city or territory, but considered themselves citizens of the world. Although the cosmopolitanism of the time gave people a sense of individualism and freedom, it also provided many with a feeling of alienation and insecurity. Old traditions and values were steadily being uprooted, static class structures were disappearing, past certitudes were questioned, and the future became uncertain. By the 2nd century c.e., the Hellenistic-Roman world had witnessed a number of barbarian invasions, political instability, and economic crises. These unsettling conditions led the people to long and search for *soteria*, salvation, liberation from the burdens of finitude, the misery and failure of human life. The feeling of alienation and escape was fostered not only by a social and political situation, but also by the new cosmology.

This new cosmology understood the world as an eternal perfect sphere composed of a system of concentric moving spheres. It was viewed as divided into two realms, translunar and sublunar, with the moon as the boundary. The translunar realm was the sphere of the heavenly bodies, the stars and the planets that move in eternal harmony. Below it was the sublunar or material world, a place of chance, corruption, and death.

Both the spiritual and the material universe were understood to be the creation of a *demiurge* or creator god. An individual was believed to be an alien wanderer in the material world. His/her true being, the soul, is immortal and belongs to the spiritual, transcendent world. Thus one's aim in life should be to purify oneself from the material things of the world and to return to his/her true home, to the world beyond, and to fellowship with the divine.

This new cosmology and view of the individual, along with the political and social situation, caused the people of the Hellenistic-Roman world to re-evaluate the local, limiting traditions with their emphasis on conformity and the gods who ordained and maintained these limits, and to reinterpret them to meet the needs of the age, the salvation of the individual, his/her deliverance or protection from the vicissitudes of this life and the perils of the afterlife. The ancient gods were hellenized and transformed from national deities to universal savior divinities, and the rites of the agricultural cults that were formerly a celebration of the seasonal drama of the land were transformed into mysteries, an experience of personal redemption. Those who were initiated into their secret rites were granted admission into fellowship with a divinity who offered them strength and support to cope with the changing world in which they lived and happiness and immortality after death. To the extent that they met the needs of the individual man and woman, both the oriental cults and those of the old gods of Greece developed and spread throughout the empire and enjoyed great appeal. The most important of all the cults was that of the oriental sun-deity Mithras, which by the end of the 2nd century c.e. had developed into an important Hellenistic mystery religion. At the beginning of the 4th century, Mithras became the official god of the Roman state, and it appeared that Mithraism might become the sole state religion. It was Constantine's acceptance of Christianity as an official religion of the empire that shattered its hopes. Much of Mithraism's influence and popularity was due to its appeal to the Roman legions, the principal agent of its dissemination, and the patronage of the imperial officials and emperors.

Mithraism and the cults enjoyed great success during the Hellenistic-Roman period. They were international and universal in character. With the exception of Mithraism, which was exclusively for men, membership in the cults was open to all regardless of sex, nationality, or race. This feature was especially appealing at a time of uncertainty and social fluidity. The cults were individualistic, addressing the spiritual needs of each person, and they provided the devotees with meaningful fellowship with individuals who held the same understanding of salvation. Lastly, they provided a personal, closer relationship to a deity who protected them from the adversities of this life, and the hope of a blissful world after death.

Philosophy also attempted to provide the same benefits. The religious philosophies that developed during this time offered to the educated minority what the cults supplied to the average individual. They were principally a way of life based on reason that offered inner security and stability. These philosophies were concerned with the "care of souls," to enable persons to function and to survive in a hostile world, and emphasized the practical and ethical matters of life rather than the metaphysical and cosmological speculations that preoccupied the philosophies of the Classical age. Their aim was the attainment of individual happiness through self-sufficiency, to free oneself from all that is external, and to live a moral and ethical life.

Judaism was also influenced by Hellenism, being transformed from a state religion into one of the most powerful and widespread of the Hellenistic religions, and from a religion of the book (the Pentateuch) to a theoretical and philosophical interpretation of its laws and customs. This was especially evident in the Judaism of the Diaspora with its center at Alexandria, the intellectual and cultural center of the empire. The Jews adopted the language of the culture as their native tongue and attempted to adjust their religious ideas to the intellectual Hellenistic viewpoint. With the adoption of Greek as their primary language, the need arose for a Greek translation of the Hebrew Scriptures to meet the religious and educational needs of Hellenistic Judaism. The translation of the Pentateuch was begun during the reign of Ptolemy II Philadelphus (282-246 B.C.E.) and was completed ca. 250. Other books of the Old Testament were gradually translated over the following two centuries. Known as the Septuagint, the Greek translation of the Hebrew Scriptures is the most significant literary achievement of the Hellenistic Jewish Diaspora. It was the main factor in the hellenization of Judaism, an important medium for transmitting the Jewish religious experience to the Hellenistic-Roman world, and it enabled Judaism to become a major world religion. The Septuagint served as the basis of all subsequent Hellenistic Jewish literature, both biblical and nonbiblical.

The hellenization of Judaism caused the Scriptures to be interpreted allegorically and to be found in them the deepest philosophical and metaphysical truths. Master of the allegorical interpretation of the Bible was the Jewish Hellenistic philosopher Philo Judaeus (ca. 20 B.C.E.–50 C.E.). Much of the Hellenistic-Jewish output at this time interpreted the Mosaic law as a code of rational ethics. Greek ideas were adopted to present Judaism as a philosophical religion in harmony with the intellectual environment of the time. This is evident in the apocalyptic and wisdom literature that developed during this period. This literature adopted and adapted the prevalent elements of Hellenistic cosmology and its view of human existence and destiny, and reflected the concerns shared by many during the Hellenistic-Roman period. Its emphasis was on the salvation of the individual and it stressed the immortality of the soul, a hereafter, and a final judgment, matters of little consequence to ancient Judaism. There was also a tendency away from nationalism toward universalism and an attempt to dissociate the worship of God from Hebrew nationalism. The message of these writings was not limited to any one nation or people; it was intended for all. God was the Lord of all people; his salvation extends to all the righteous, and his judgments will fall upon all the wicked.

The influence of Hellenistic Judaism began to wane after the destruction of the temple and Jerusalem in 70 C.E. At that time, Judaism came under the influence and power of the rabbis, who rejected Hellenistic Judaism's philosophical interpretation of the law and its apocalyptic views and wisdom theology. Judaism returned to the strict devotion to the law and the Scriptures. By the middle of the 4th century, Hellenistic Judaism all but ceased to exist. The Judaism that survived and developed was rabbinic Judaism.

Two other new religious systems of thought, Christianity and Gnosticism, developed during the Hellenistic-Roman age. Christianity originated as a subgroup within Palestinian Judaism, formed by a small group of Jesus' followers who had witnessed his resurrection and interpreted it to signify him as the long-awaited Messiah. Christianity was introduced into the gentile Hellenistic world by Hellenistic Jews, who encountered Christianity on their pilgrimages to the Jerusalem temple during the high holy days. As a product of the times, Christianity shared the soteriological goals and ethical concerns of the cults, religions, and religious philosophies. Initially a movement of the disinherited, the poor, and uneducated, by the mid-2nd century Christianity had attracted individuals from all walks of life. It attracted in particular serious students of philosophy who had become disenchanted with the various philosophical schools. Christianity's major appeal was the social and psychological benefits that it provided to its adherents, benefits not found in the cults or philosophies. It was open to all with no restrictions other than steadfastness to the faith. The cults tended to be secretive, exclusive, and their initiation rites often expensive, and the religious philosophies required some degree of education and made salvation an intellectual accomplishment. Christianity's most important benefit was its sense of community that was not found in any cult or philosophy. It offered its members a true sense of belonging, a sense of security. The Christian community was close-knit, organized, and disciplined and was concerned with every aspect of each member's life, ready to give whatever assistance one needed in any situation. Its creed was based on love of all humanity, and its charity and philanthropy were universal. This was a major factor in its growth and success.

Yet despite its appeal, Christianity was not readily accepted into the Hellenistic-Roman social world. As it gained adherents, it also gained critics, both from the Roman authorities and the pagan intellectuals. The Christians refused to pay proper homage to the state gods that were considered the protective force of the Roman state, and their refusal to bear arms and to participate in civic life was viewed as seditious. By the 2nd century, the Christians' neglect of the gods was believed to be the cause of the calamities that had befallen the empire, and provoked major persecutions against them and the rise of anti-Christian polemics. In defending Christianity against its critics, Christian intellectuals, beginning in the late 2nd century, sought to establish Christianity as a philosophy, a way of life comparable to the contemporary philosophical schools that by then had developed into a religion based on reason. Christianity's conflicts with the Roman state and its intellectuals and, during the 2nd and 3rd centuries, its internal conflict with Gnosticism caused it to establish an organized ecclesiastical hierarchy, define and explain its beliefs, and to systematize them. This led to the establishment of a standardized scriptural canon based on apostolic authority, and the development of an authoritative creed and a distinctive Christian theology. By the early 4th century, Christianity had become the most effectively organized and disciplined body within the empire, independent and self-sufficient. These factors were important in establishing Christianity as the religion of the empire.

The last major religious movement to develop during this period was Gnosticism. It was not a uniform religion, but a view of the universe and the individual promulgated in various groups or sects within Judaism,

Christianity, and paganism. Gnosticism flourished during the 2nd and 3rd centuries c.e., and was most prominent within Christianity. Although widely divergent and disunited, there existed among the Gnostics' systems certain common concepts, principal of which was the unique understanding of *gnosis*, a revealed knowledge through which the individual's salvation is achieved. Similar to many of the religious ideas that arose during the Hellenistic-Roman period, Gnosticism was fostered by the transient conditions, continuing sufferings, and misfortunes of the time that created in individuals a sense of insecurity and alienation. Their solutions to these conditions were the most radical and extreme of all the contemporary religious thoughts. The Gnostics advocated the rejection of the created world, its creator, despots, and rulers, and through *gnosis*, which only they could possess, the return to the world of light and the true supreme unknown God, the only god that they acknowledged.

Gnosis provided the Gnostics with an understanding of their divine nature, of God, of whom they are a spark, of the nature of the world, of the purpose and destiny of humankind, and freed them from all worldly constraints. Liberated from the material world with its social, moral, and legal controls, the Gnostics determined their own behavioral patterns. Their social and ethical conduct was either ascetic or libertine. Although extreme opposites, both asceticism and libertinism expressed the same fundamental attitude, the rejection of the world and its laws — asceticism through abstinence and libertinism through excess.

The Gnostics considered themselves an "elite" group, the spiritual members of humankind, and the only ones capable of redemption. Everyone else was either a *psychikos*, one who possessed soul and free will, but lacked the enlightenment of the spiritual and thus could not attain the realm of light, or a *hylikos*, one who was dominated by the carnal element and was spiritually ignorant. Membership in an elite group provided the Gnostics with a feeling of security in an insecure world as well as a sense of superiority. However, Gnosticism's solutions to the issues confronting humankind were inadequate for the average individual. They were too extreme and contrary to the traditional view of the world and humanity's place and destiny in it. These factors and its lack of organization were major causes of Gnosticism's demise.

The Hellenistic-Roman era was a religious age with a common longing and search for personal salvation, liberation from the burdens of finitude, and the hope of a blessed afterlife through knowledge of one's origin,

identity, and destiny. Old and new cults, religious philosophies, and the religions of the time — Judaism, Christianity, and Gnosticism — attempted
to fulfill this need. There was also a strong tendency toward the belief in a
single deity. This was evident in Judaism, which claimed that the national
god, Yahweh, was the god of all, and in the cults, where the various divine
names — Isis, Cybele, Mithras, or others — were designations of the same
single, supreme deity. With the exception of Epicureanism, the religious
philosophies also advocated a supreme cosmic power. The Stoics called it
the Logos, Divine Reason, or God, and the Middle Platonists called it the
One, the Good, or God. The Hellenistic-Roman religious age came to an
end in the 4th century. In 324, the emperor Constantine accepted Christianity as an official religion of the empire and became its generous patron,
and in 380, Emperor Theodosius I proclaimed it the official religion of the
empire. All pagan worship was outlawed in an edict of 391. Christianity's
strength and official status within the empire contributed to Gnosticism's
disappearance. Judaism continued to develop as rabbinic Judaism.

The situation of the world today is not very different from that of the
Hellenistic-Roman world. Individuals are faced with many of the same issues and search for *soteria*, the general betterment of life, and a sense of
identity. Technological advances in communication and travel have
blurred the boundaries between countries, and the Internet has almost
created the *oikoumene*, the single world community of Alexander the
Great that simultaneously contains many individual cultures. These advances, although beneficial to humankind, have raised concerns in individuals about their identity, purpose, and the meaning of life. To meet the
needs of the time, cults have evolved and have become very popular, as has
new religious thought, e.g., the New Age movement and Neo-paganism.
Times and circumstances have changed, but the concerns of the Hellenistic-Roman age and their possible solutions can still be found in today's
world.

BIBLIOGRAPHY

Chapter I. The Hellenistic-Roman World

General Studies

Angus, Samuel. *The Religious Quest of the Greco-Roman World.* New York: Biblo and Tannen, 1967.

Bell, H. Idris. *Cults and Creeds in Graeco-Roman Egypt.* New York: Philosophical Library, 1953.

Dodds, E. R. *Pagan and Christian in an Age of Anxiety.* New York: W. W. Norton, 1970.

Ferguson, John. *The Religions of the Roman Empire.* Ithaca: Cornell University Press, 1970.

Fraser, P. M. *Ptolemaic Alexandria.* 3 vols. Oxford: Oxford University Press, 1972.

Grant, Frederick C. *Hellenistic Religions: The Age of Syncretism.* New York: Liberal Arts, 1953.

Grant, Michael. *From Alexander to Cleopatra: The Hellenistic World.* New York: Charles Scribner's Sons, 1982.

Green, Peter. *Alexander of Macedonia, 356-323 B.C.: A Historical Biography.* Berkeley: University of California Press, 1991.

Hadas, Moses. *Hellenistic Culture: Fusion and Diffusion.* 1959, repr. New York: W. W. Norton, 1972.

Koester, Helmut. *Introduction to the New Testament.* 1: *History, Culture and Religion of the Hellenistic Age.* Philadelphia: Fortress, 1982.

Martin, Luther H. *Hellenistic Religions: An Introduction.* New York: Oxford University Press, 1987.

Momigliano, Arnaldo. *On Pagans, Jews and Christians.* Middletown: Wesleyan University Press, 1987.

Neusner, Jacob, ed. *Christianity, Judaism and Other Greco-Roman Cults.* 2: *Early Christianity.* Leiden: E. J. Brill, 1975.

Nilsson, Martin P. "The New Conception of the Universe in Late Greek Paganism." *Eranos* 44 (1946), 20-27.

Rostovtzeff, M. I. *Social and Economic History of the Hellenistic World.* 3 vols. Oxford: Clarendon, 1941.

Smith, Jonathan Z. *Drudgery Divine: On the Comparison of Early Christianity and the Religions of Late Antiquity.* Chicago: University of Chicago Press, 1990.

———. *Map Is Not Territory: Studies in the History of Religions.* SJLA 23. Leiden: E. J. Brill, 1978.

Tarn, William W., and G. T. Griffith. *Hellenistic Civilization.* 3rd ed. Cleveland: World, 1966.

Walbank, F. W. *The Hellenistic World.* Rev. ed. Cambridge, Mass.: Harvard University Press, 1993.

Welles, C. Bradford. *Alexander and the Hellenistic World.* Toronto: A. M. Hakkert, 1970.

The Mystery Cults

Allen, T. W., and E. E. Sikes, eds. *The Homeric Hymns.* New York: Macmillan, 1904.

Burkert, Walter. *Greek Religion.* Cambridge, Mass.: Harvard University Press, 1985.

Cole, Susan Guettel. "New Evidence for the Mysteries of Dionysos." *GRBS* 21 (1980): 223-38.

Cumont, Franz. *After Life in Roman Paganism.* New York: Dover, 1959.

Gasparro, Giulia Sfameni. *Soteriology and Mystic Aspects in the Cult of Cybele and Attis.* EPRO 103. Leiden: E. J. Brill, 1985.

Grenfell, Bernard P., and Arthur S. Hunt, eds. *The Oxyrhynchus Papyri* XI 1380. London: Egyptian Exploration Society, 1915.

Griffiths, J. Gwyn, ed. *The Isis-Book (Metamorphoses, Book XI)/Apuleius of Madauros.* EPRO 39. Leiden: E. J. Brill, 1975.

Heyob, Sharon Kelly. *The Cult of Isis Among Women in the Graeco-Roman World*. EPRO 51. Leiden: E. J. Brill, 1975.

Kerényi, C. *Dionysos: Archetypal Image of Indestructible Life*. Bollingen Series 65, vol. 2. Princeton: Princeton University Press, 1976.

Mylonas, George E. *Eleusis and the Eleusinian Mysteries*. Princeton: Princeton University Press, 1961.

Nilsson, Martin P. *The Dionysiac Mysteries of the Hellenistic and Roman Age*. New York: Arno, 1975.

————. *Greek Folk Religion*. New York: Harper, 1961.

Otto, Walter F. *Dionysus, Myth and Cult*. Bloomington: Indiana University Press, 1965.

Richardson, N. J., ed. *The Homeric Hymn to Demeter*. Oxford: Clarendon, 1974.

Showerman, Grant. *The Great Mother of the Gods*. Chicago: Argonaut, 1969.

Solmsen, Friedrich. *Isis among the Greeks and Romans*. Cambridge, Mass.: Harvard University Press, 1979.

Vermaseren, Maarten J. *Cybele and Attis: the Myth and the Cult*. London: Thames and Hudson, 1977.

Witt, R. E. *Isis in the Graeco-Roman World*. Ithaca: Cornell University Press, 1971.

Religious Philosophies

Armstrong, A. H. *Introduction to Ancient Philosophy*. Boston: Beacon, 1963.

————, ed. *The Cambridge History of Later Greek and Early Medieval Philosophy*. Cambridge: Cambridge University Press, 1967.

Farrington, Benjamin. *The Faith of Epicurus*. London: Weidenfeld and Nicolson, 1967.

Festugière, A.-J. *Epicurus and His Gods*. Oxford: Blackwell, 1955.

Hicks, Robert Drew. *Stoic and Epicurean*. 1910, repr. New York: Russell & Russell, 1962.

Kristeller, Paul Oskar. *Greek Philosophers of the Hellenistic Age*. New York: Columbia University Press, 1993.

Long, A. A. and D. N. Sedley, eds. *The Hellenistic Philosophers. 1: Translations of Principal Sources with Philosophical Commentary*. Cambridge: Cambridge University Press, 1987.

Sandbach, F. H. *The Stoics*. New York: Norton, 1975.

Chapter II. Mithraism

Beck, Roger. "Mithraism since Franz Cumont." *ANRW* 17/4: 2002-2115. New York: Walter de Gruyter, 1984.

Burkert, Walter. *Ancient Mystery Cults*. Cambridge, Mass.: Harvard University Press, 1987.

Cumont, Franz. *After Life in Roman Paganism*. New York: Dover, 1959.

————. *The Mysteries of Mithra*. New York: Dover, 1956.

Gager, John G. *Kingdom and Community: The Social World of Early Christianity*. Englewood Cliffs: Prentice-Hall, 1975.

Gordon, R. L. "Mithraism and Roman Society." *Religion* 2 (1978), 92-121.

————. "Reality, evocation and boundary in the Mysteries of Mithras." *JMS* 3 (1980): 19-99.

Hinnells, John R., ed. *Mithraic Studies: Proceedings of the First International Congress of Mithraic Studies*. 2 vols. Manchester: Manchester University Press, 1975.

Merkelbach, Reinhold. *Mithras*. Königstein: Hain, 1984.

Nock, Arthur Darby. "The Genius of Mithraism." *JRS* 27 (1937).

Patterson, Leonard. *Mithraism and Christianity: A Study in Comparative Religion*. Cambridge: Cambridge University Press, 1921.

Speidel, Michael P. *Mithras-Orion: Greek Hero and Roman Army God*. EPRO 81. Leiden: E. J. Brill, 1980.

Turcan, Robert. *Mithras Platonicus*. EPRO 47. Leiden: E. J. Brill, 1975.

Ulansey, David. *The Origins of the Mithraic Mysteries: Cosmology and Salvation in the Ancient World*. New York: Oxford University Press, 1989.

Vermaseren, M J. *Mithras, the Secret God*. New York: Barnes & Noble, 1963.

Wynne-Tyson, Esmé. *Mithras: The Fellow in the Cap*. 2nd ed. New York: Barnes & Noble, 1972.

Chapter III. Hellenistic Judaism

Bentwich, Norman. *Hellenism*. Philadelphia: Jewish Publication Society of America, 1919.

Bickerman, Elias J. *The Jews in the Greek Age*. Cambridge, Mass.: Harvard University Press, 1988.

————. *Studies in Jewish and Christian History*. AGJU 9/1. Leiden: E. J. Brill, 1976.

Boccaccini, Gabriele. *Middle Judaism: Jewish Thought, 300 B.C.E. to 200 C.E.* Minneapolis: Fortress, 1991.

Charlesworth, James H., ed. *The Old Testament Pseudepigrapha.* 2 vols. Garden City: Doubleday, 1985.

Colson, F. H., G. H. Whitaker, and R. Marcus, eds. *Philo.* 12 vols. Loeb Classical Library. New York: Putnam, 1929-1962.

Davies, W. D., and Louis Finkelstein, eds. *The Cambridge History of Judaism.* 3 vols. Cambridge: Cambridge University Press, 1984-99.

Feldman, Louis H. *Jew and Gentile in the Ancient World: Attitudes and Interactions from Alexander to Justinian.* Princeton: Princeton University Press, 1993.

Gordis, Robert. *Koheleth — The Man and His World.* 3rd ed. New York: Schocken, 1968.

Grant, Michael. *The Jews in the Roman World.* New York: Barnes & Noble, 1995.

Green, William Scott, ed. *Approaches to Ancient Judaism.* 4: *Studies in Liturgy, Exegesis, and Talmudic Narrative.* Brown Judaic Studies 27. Chico: Scholars, 1983.

Gutmann, Joseph, comp. *The Synagogue: Studies in Origins, Archaeology and Architecture.* New York: Ktav, 1975.

———, ed. *Ancient Synagogues: The State of Research.* Brown Judaic Studies 22. Chico: Scholars, 1981.

Hadas, Moses. *Hellenistic Culture: Fusion and Diffusion.* 1959, repr. New York: W. W. Norton, 1972.

———, ed. *Aristeas to Philocrates.* 1951, repr. New York: Ktav, 1973.

Hanson, Paul D. *The Dawn of Apocalyptic.* Rev. ed. Philadelphia: Fortress, 1979.

Hengel, Martin. *Jews, Greeks, and Barbarians: Aspects of the Hellenization of Judaism in the Pre-Christian Period.* Philadelphia: Fortress, 1980.

———. *Judaism and Hellenism: Studies in Their Encounter in Palestine During the Early Hellenistic Period.* 2 vols. Philadelphia: Fortress, 1974.

———. *The "Hellenization" of Judaea in the First Century after Christ.* Philadelphia: Trinity, 1989.

Koch, Klaus. *The Rediscovery of Apocalyptic.* SBT, 2nd 22. Naperville: Alec R. Allenson, 1972.

Levine, Lee I., ed. *The Synagogue in Late Antiquity.* Philadelphia: American Schools of Oriental Research, 1987.

Newsome, James D. *Greeks, Romans, Jews: Currents of Culture and Belief in the New Testament World.* Philadelphia: Trinity, 1992.

Russell, D. S. *The Method and Message of Jewish Apocalyptic, 200 B.C.–A.D. 100.* OTL. Philadelphia: Westminister, 1964.

Safrai, S., and M. Stern, eds. *The Jewish People in the First Century.* 2 vols. Amsterdam: Van Gorcum, 1976.

Sanders, E. P. *Judaism: Practice and Belief 63 B.C.E.–66 C.E.* Philadelphia: Trinity, 1992.

Sandmel, Samuel. *Judaism and Christian Beginnings.* New York: Oxford University Press, 1978.

Schürer, Emil. *The History of the Jewish People in the Age of Jesus Christ.* Rev. ed. 3 vols. Edinburgh: T. & T. Clark, 1973-1987.

Stone, Michael E., ed. *Jewish Writings of the Second Temple Period.* CRINT 2/2. Philadelphia: Fortress, 1984.

Sukenik, E. L. *Ancient Synagogues in Palestine and Greece.* 1934, repr. Munich: Kraus, 1980.

Tcherikover, Victor. *Hellenistic Civilization and the Jews.* 1959, repr. New York: Atheneum, 1970.

———, ed. *Corpus Papyrorum Judaicarum.* Vol. 1. Cambridge, Mass.: Harvard University Press, 1957.

Tripolitis, Antonía. *The Doctrine of the Soul in the Thought of Plotinus and Origen.* Roslyn Heights, N.Y.: Libra, 1978.

von Rad, Gerhard. *Wisdom in Israel.* Nashville: Abingdon, 1972.

Whybray, R. N. *Wisdom in Proverbs.* SBT 45. Naperville: Alec R. Allenson, 1965.

Wilken, Robert L., ed. *Aspects of Wisdom in Judaism and Early Christianity.* Studies in Judaism and Christianity in Antiquity 1. Notre Dame: University of Notre Dame Press, 1975.

Williamson, Ronald. *Jews in the Hellenistic World: Philo.* Cambridge: Cambridge University Press, 1989.

Zeitlin, Solomon. "The Origin of the Synagogue." *American Academy for Jewish Research, Proceedings 1930-31.* New York: Kraus, 1968, 66-81.

Chapter IV. Christianity

Andresen, Carl. *Logos und Nomos: Die Polemic des Kelsos wider das Christentum.* Berlin: Walter de Gruyter, 1955.

Benko, Stephen. "Pagan Chriticism of Christianity During the First Two Centuries." *ANRW* 2, 23/2. Ed. by H. Temporini and W. Haase. Berlin: Walter de Gruyter, 1980, 1054-1118.

———. *Pagan Rome and the Early Christians.* Bloomington: Indiana University Press, 1984.

———, and John J. O'Rourke. *The Catacombs and the Colosseum: The Roman Empire as the Setting of Primitive Christianity.* Valley Forge: Judson, 1971.

Burtchaell, James T. *From Synagogue to Church: Public Services and Offices in the Earliest Christian Communities.* Cambridge: Cambridge University Press, 1992.

von Campenhausen, Hans. *Tradition and Life in the Church: Essays and Lectures in Church History.* Philadelphia: Fortress, 1968.

Chadwick, Henry, trans. *Origen: Contra Celsum.* 1965, repr. Cambridge: Cambridge University Press, 1980.

Davies, A. Powell. *The First Christian: A Study of St. Paul and Christian Origins.* New York: Farrar, Straus and Cudahy, 1957.

Doran, Robert. *Birth of a Worldview: Early Christianity in its Jewish and Pagan Context.* Boulder: Westview, 1995.

Frend, W. H. C. *The Rise of Christianity.* Philadelphia: Fortress, 1984.

Gager, John G. *Kingdom and Community: The Social World of Early Christianity.* Englewood Cliffs: Prentice-Hall, 1975.

Grant, Robert M. *Augustus to Constantine: The Thrust of the Christian Movement into the Roman World.* New York: Harper & Row, 1970.

Hazlett, Ian, ed. *Early Christianity: Origins and Evolution to A.D. 600.* London: SPCK, 1991.

Hexter, J. H. *The Judaeo-Christian Tradition.* 2nd ed. New Haven: Yale University Press, 1995.

Koetschau, Paul, ed. *Origenes Werkes.* Die Griechischen Christlichen Schriftsteller der Ersten Drei Jahrhunderte 2/1-12: Leipzig: J. C. Hinrichs, 1891-1955.

Ladner, Gerhart B. *God, Cosmos and Humankind: The World of Early Christian Symbolism.* Berkeley: University of California Press, 1995.

Lane Fox, Robin. *Pagans and Christians.* 1987, repr. San Francisco: HarperSanFrancisco, 1995.

Lommatzsch, C. H. E. *Origen Opera Omnia.* 25 vols. Berlin: Sumtibus Haude et Spener, 1831-1848.

MacMullen, Ramsay. *Christianizing the Roman Empire A.D. 100-400.* New Haven: Yale University Press, 1984.

Meeks, Wayne A. *The First Urban Christians: The Social World of the Apostle Paul.* New Haven: Yale University Press, 1983.

Musurillo, Herbert A., ed. *The Fathers of the Primitive Church.* New York: New American Library, 1966.

Nock, Arthur Darby. *Conversion: The Old and New in Religion from Alexander the Great to Augustine of Hippo.* 1933, repr. Baltimore: Johns Hopkins University Press, 1998.

———. *Early Gentile Christianity and its Hellenistic Background.* New York: Harper & Row, 1964.

Roberts, Alexander, and James Donaldson, eds. *Ante-Nicene Fathers* 1-2, 8. Grand Rapids: Wm. B. Eerdmans, 1979.

Ruiz Bueno, Daniel, ed. *Padres Apologistas Griegos.* Madrid: La Editorial Catolica, 1954.

Smith, Jonathan Z. *Drudgery Divine: On the Comparison of Early Christianities and the Religions of Late Antiquity.* Chicago: University of Chicago Press, 1990.

Tripolitis, Antonía. *Origen: A Critical Reading.* New York: Peter Lang, 1985.

Wilken, Robert L. *The Christians as the Romans Saw Them.* New Haven: Yale University Press, 1984.

Chapter V. Gnosticism

Blackman, Edwin C. *Marcion and His Influence.* London: SPCK, 1948.

Dodd, C. H. *The Bible and the Greeks.* London: Hodder & Stoughton, 1935.

Filoramo, Giovanni. *A History of Gnosticism.* Cambridge, Mass.: Blackwell, 1994.

Grant, Robert M. *Gnosticism and Early Christianity.* Rev. ed. New York: Harper & Row, 1966.

Green, Henry Alan. "Suggested Sociological Themes in the Study of Gnosticism." *VC* 31 (1977), 169-80.

———. *The Economic and Social Origins of Gnosticism.* SBLDS 77. Atlanta: Scholars, 1985.

Haardt, Robert. *Gnosis: Character and Testimony.* Leiden: E. J. Brill, 1971.

———. *Marcion: The Gospel of the Alien God.* Durham, N.C.: Labyrinth, 1990.

Hermetica. Tran. by Brian P. Copenhaver. Cambridge: Cambridge University Press, 1992.

Hippolytus. *Refutatio omnium haeresium.* Ed. by Paul Wendland. Die Griechischen Christlichen Schriftsteller der Ersten Drei Jahrhunderte 3. Leipzig: Hinrichs, 1916.

Irenaeus. *Adversus haereses.* Ed. by W. W. Harvey. Cambridge: Cambridge University Press, 1857.

Jonas, Hans. *The Gnostic Religion.* 2nd ed. Boston: Beacon, 1963.

Knox, John. *Marcion and the New Testament.* Chicago: University of Chicago Press, 1942.

Layton, Bentley. *The Gnostic Scriptures.* Garden City: Doubleday, 1987.

Nock, Arthur Darby. "Gnosticism." *HTR* 57 (1964): 255-79.

————, and A.-J. Festugière, eds. *Corpus Hermeticum* 1-4. Paris: Les Belles Lettres, 1945-1954.

Pagels, Elaine. *The Gnostic Gospels.* New York: Random House, 1979.

Robinson, James M., ed. *The Nag Hammadi Library in English.* 3rd ed. San Francisco: Harper & Row, 1988.

Rudolph, Kurt. *Gnosis: The Nature and History of Gnosticism.* San Francisco: Harper & Row, 1987.

Tertullian. *Adversus Marcionem.* 2 vols. Ed. and trans. by Ernest Evans. Oxford: Clarendon, 1972.

————. *Adversus Valentinanos.* Ed. by A. Kroyman. Corpus Scriptorum Ecclesiasticorum Latinorum 47. Leipzig: G. Freytag, 1906.

von Harnack, Adolf. *Marcion: Das Evangelium vom Fremden Gott,* 2nd ed. Leipzig: J. C. Hinrichs, 1924.

Walker, Benjamin. *Gnosticism: Its History and Influence.* Northhamptonshire: Aquarian, 1983.

INDEX